SPEAK JAMAICAN
A Guide To Fluency

I'Heshia Handy

SPEAK JAMAICAN
A Guide To Fluency

Cover Image Designer: I'Heshia Handy
Cover Image Creator: Garry Hamilton

ISBN-10: 0692046100
ISBN-13: 978-0692046104
Library of Congress Control Number: 2018900044

Acknowledgements
The author would like to thank family and friends for their support and encouragement of the endeavor to undertake this project. Special thanks to: Shantana Dyer, Camille Green-Wright, Nerissa Noad, Elva Rose, Oshane Sinclair, Byanka White, and Alexia Wright.

Contents

Introduction i
Author's Notes iii
Abbreviations Used In This Book v
Contractions Used In Jamaican Creole vii

LESSON ONE 1
   Pronunciation i
   Diphthongs. 2
   Additional Rules Of Jamaican Creole 3

LESSON TWO 8
   Jamaican Creole Grammar. 8
   The Simple Present Tense. 8

LESSON THREE 11
   Present Conjugation Of The Verb Bi 11

LESSON FOUR 16
   The Present Continuous Tense 16

LESSON FIVE 20
   Pluralizing 20
   Pluralizing Indefinite Adjectives And
   Adjectives Of Quantity. 20
   Pluralizing Demonstrative Adjectives .21
   Pluralizing Adjectives Demonstrating Possession 23

Pluralizing Nouns 23
Pluralizing Personal Pronouns. 26
Pluralizing Demonstrative Pronouns. 28
Pluralizing Indefinite Pronouns 28

LESSON SIX 31
The Simple Past Tense 31

LESSON SEVEN 36
The Case Of The Verb Bi In The Simple Past Tense 36

LESSON EIGHT 41
The Continuous Past Tense. 41

LESSON NINE 44
The Present Perfect Tense 44
The Continuous Present Perfect Tense 47

LESSON TEN 50
The Past Perfect Tense 50
The Continuous Past Perfect Tense 52

LESSON ELEVEN 54
The Future Tense. 54
The Conditional Future Tense. 57

LESSON TWELVE. 63
When A Verb Phrase Contains An Infinitive 63

LESSON THIRTEEN 70
The Passive Voice. 70
The Impersonal Passive Voice 71

LESSON FOURTEEN. 77
Making A Sentence Negative 77
Negative Auxiliary Verbs. 77
The Negative Passive Voice 88
The Negative Modal Auxiliary Verbs 88
The Remaining Modal Auxiliary Verbs 91
The Double Negative Structure Of Jamaican Creole 92

LESSON FIFTEEN 96
Asking Questions 96

LESSON SIXTEEN 101
Showing Ownership 101
The Possessive Pronouns 101
Adjectives Demonstrating Possession 102
The Possessive Nouns 103

LESSON SEVENTEEN 106
Forming Adjectives And Adverbs 106

LESSON EIGHTEEN 113
Da, Datdeh, Dat, Seh, And Weh 113

LESSON NINTEEN 117
The Tendency To Use Goh And Come After Verbs Of
Movement 117

LESSON TWENTY 122
Commands 122
Repetition Of Nouns, Pronouns, And Verbs 124
The Use Of A And Fi 125
The Use Of Ku 125
The Use Of Fi And Fa 125
The Case Of Kyah And Kyaah 126
Gender 126

LESSON TWENTY-ONE 128
Putting It All Together 128
Reading Comprehension 1 128
Reading Comprehension 2 129
Frequently Asked Questions 131
Commonly Used Expressions 133
Frequently Used Jamaican Proverbs 135
Appendix 137
Tenses Of Jamaican Creole Verbs 137
References 157

Introduction

It has been a long wait, but now here is a bona fide Jamaican Creole teaching tool. This is a course designed for people who wish to speak fluent Jamaican Creole. Jamaican Creole is spoken on a continuum, ranging from what many Jamaicans would regard as 'raw patois' to almost English. The more formal the setting, the more likely the language is to be closer to English. This book is intended to teach Jamaican Creole in its truest form. It should be noted that Jamaican Creole can vary to a small extent when spoken in different parts of the island. This is taken into account when addressing the tenses of Jamaican Creole.

Jamaican Creole, as were many other dialects, was born out of practicality. When West African people were brought to the West Indies to work as slaves over three hundred and fifty years ago, they spoke many different languages (Gladwell, 1994). This posed a problem for the people to communicate effectively. To compound the issue, the language disparity was even engineered on various plantations by plantation owners to ensure that rebellions would be kept to a minimum. They practiced putting people of different African tribes together to impede communication (Madden, 2009). Inevitably, a dialect emerged from this quagmire. This situation was not unique to Jamaica, as many of the other islands colonized by the English and other European countries also developed dialects.

i

As a result of the history of Jamaica, the dialect has been influenced by West African languages in the Gold Coast and Congo regions of Africa (Gladwell, 1994). Words such as *pikni/pikini* and *nyam* are often referenced by Jamaicans to be of West African origin. The influences of these languages are not predominantly seen in the words themselves, which are predominantly English-derived words, but in the structure of sentences. They echo the patterns of these West African languages. The tendency to reduplicate words originated from West African languages (Cassidy, 1957). Interestingly, some words are similar to Spanish words and are used in the same contexts. Two such words are *mi* and *a*. Jamaica was once colonized by the Spaniards, but it is doubtful that this is the origin of these words.

The differences between English and Jamaican Creole are most evident in words with changeable forms such as verbs, adjectives, adverbs, and the syntax or arrangement of these words in sentences. It is the expectation that the reader will demonstrate fluency in speech after completing this course.

Author's Notes

Before one can fully understand a language, one must learn its grammar and its phonology. In subsequent sections, you will encounter lessons that will help you to understand Jamaican Creole sentence structure, verb conjugation, adjective formation, adverb formation, making sentences negative, showing ownership, language patterns unique to Jamaican Creole, and additional tenets of Jamaican Creole. It is important to note that Jamaican Creole is not a formal language. As such, there might be a variety of spellings for a particular word when it is written by different people. What the author did was to use the simplest spelling for each syllable of a word so as to imitate as best as possible the spoken word. The words most commonly used in everyday conversation are used in the examples and exercises included in this book.

It is important to pay attention to the pronunciation key that follows, as words may resemble some English words but are not pronounced the same way. They may also not have the same meaning. There are certain words that are pronounced slightly differently in Jamaican Creole than they are in English. These words are included as if they were bona fide Jamaican Creole words. An example of this is Jamaican Creole *daag*, with English equivalent *dog*.

The meanings of some Jamaican Creole sentences or ideas are contextual. That is to say, additional meaning is inferred from the broader setting or context within which the ideas are stated. For example, *Mi goh a Spalding* is literally translated *I go to Spalding*. Within a certain context, however, the sentence can actually mean *I went to Spalding*. That might sound a little complicated now, but it will become clear once you go through the lessons.

Abbreviations Used In This Book

adj.	adjective
adv.	adverb
adv. phrase	adverb phrase
conj.	conjunction
contr.	contraction
E.	English
interj.	interjection
JC.	Jamaican Creole
lit.	literally
mod. aux.	modal auxiliary verb
n.	noun
n/a	not applicable
plur.	plural
prep.	preposition
pron.	pronoun

sing.	singular
uncontr.	uncontracted
v.	verb
v. phrase	verb phrase

Contractions Used In Jamaican Creole

Certain contractions used in English are excluded in Jamaican Creole, while some used in Jamaican Creole are not used in English. The following list includes contractions used in Jamaican Creole along with their uncontracted meanings and English meanings.

JC. Contr.	Uncontr. Meaning	English Meaning
aggo	a goh	is going
anno	a noh	is not
dideh	deh deh; bi deh	am/is/are there; be there
didehsoh	deh dehsoh	is there; are there
dwiit	duh ih/duh it	do it
fihit	fi it	for it; its
fiit	fi it	for it; its
gaa	goh a	go to
giim	gi him/gi im	give him
gimmi	gi mi	give me; give it to me

JC. Contr.	Uncontr. Meaning	English Meaning
gwaan	goh aan	go on
haffi	ha fi	have to
indeh	inna deh	in there
inna'ih	inna di	in the
leggo	let goh	let go
miit	mi ih/mi it	me it (*e.g., Gi miit (E. Give me it)*)
neev'n	not iiv'n/noh iiv'n	not even; does not even; do not even; did not even; has not even; have not even
neev'n did	not iiv'n did/noh iiv'n did	did not even; had not even
niiv'n	not iiv'n/noh iiv'n	not even; does not even; do not even; did not even; has not even; have not even
niiv'n did	not iiv'n did/noh iiv'n did	did not even; had not even
noffi	noh fi	ought not to; should not
pudong	put dong	put down
siim	si him/si im	see him
siit	si ih/si it	see it
sisso	seh soh	say so
waa	wa a	what is
wii	wi wi	we will
y'a	yuh a	you are

Lesson One

Pronunciation

The alphabet of Jamaican Creole is the same as the English alphabet (except the letter û which was added for practical reasons), and the letters predominantly have the same pronunciations. Unlike in English, however, each letter of the Jamaican Creole alphabet has a set, distinct sound. An example of this is *c*. It is always hard in Jamaican Creole, unlike in English where it can take on a *c* or an *s* sound. Consider the words *cat* and *cease*.

Pay careful attention to the specific pronunciation of each syllable, as the word may look like an English word but is pronounced differently in Jamaican Creole. It may also have a different meaning. An example of this is the Jamaican Creole word *dot* (E. *dirt*). It is spelled like the English word *dot* meaning *spot* (which is also used by Jamaicans in the same context), but the *o* is pronounced like the 'o' sound in *dove*.

Jamaican Creole diphthongs also have consistent and distinct sounds. A guide to the pronunciation of vowel sounds and consonants follows with an example of a word imitating the sound. Unless otherwise stated, the pronunciations are as follows. Refer to them as often as is necessary.

1

Vowels

a- sharp *a*, as in r*a*p

e- sharp *e*, as in b*e*t

i- sharp *i*, as in z*i*p

o- sharp *o*, as in d*o*ve

u- sharp *u*, as in p*u*t

û- pronounced like the *i* in th*i*rd and the *u* in m*u*rder

Consonants

C is pronounced like English *k*, except before *h*.

Ch is pronounced like the *ch* in *ch*icken.

G is pronounced like the *g* in g*e*t before and after vowels. After consonants, it has a softer sound much like the *g* in ba*ng*.

S is pronounced like the *s* in *s*ee.

Consonant combinations are generally used as they are in English, e.g., *ng*, *rt*, *nk*, *nt*, etc. The exception is *ph*, where *p* and *h* have distinct sounds when used in Jamaican Creole.

Diphthongs

Diphthongs are pronounced as a single syllable.

aa- pronounced like the long *a* sound in p*a*th

ai- pronounced like *ai* in T*ai*wan

au- pronounced like *au* in *au*gment

ay- pronounced like *ay* in *ay*e

ee- pronounced like *a* in spr*a*y

ia- pronounced like the *ia* in Gamb*ia*

ii- pronounced like the *ee* in qu*ee*n

oo- pronounced like the long *o* sound in fl*o*at

ou- pronounced like *ou* in *out*

ua- pronounced like *ua* in G*ua*temala

uo- pronounced uh-wo

uu- pronounced like the *oo* sound in afterno*oo*n

ya- pronounced like the *ya* in *ya*p

ye- pronounced like the *ye* is *ye*s

yu- pronounced like *ew* sound in neph*ew* or like *you* in *you*th

Jamaican Creole utilizes a sizeable proportion of English words. These words are generally pronounced as they are in English. Words that are pronounced slightly differently in Jamaican Creole are spelled with the Jamaican Creole alphabet. Please note that words that are indicated to be English (identified with the abbreviation E.), but have an additional meaning when used in Jamaican Creole, are pronounced as in English.

Additional Rules Of Jamaican Creole

The 'th' Sound

It should be noted that the 'th' sound is absent in Jamaican Creole and is replaced by the 't' sound in most cases. Some examples are *tûrmos, tyeta,* and *tonda* (E. *thermos, theater,* and *thunder*).

In the case of a small number of words (primarily pronouns and adverbs), the 'd' sound is used exclusively to replace the 'th' sound at the beginning of words. Some examples include *dyer, den, duoz, dis, dat, dem, demself, dan, di, diiz,* and *deeh* (E. *there, then, those, this, that, them, themselves, than, the, these,* and *they*).

When 'th' occurs between two vowels, the 'd' sound frequently replaces it. Some examples are *wedda, faada,* and *bredda* (E. *weather, father,* and *brother*). When 'th' occurs at the end of a word, it is usually replaced by 't'. An example of this is *paat* (E. *path*). An exception to this is *wid* (E. *with*).

3

The 'R' Sound

The letter 'r' is usually only pronounced when it occurs at the beginning or at the end of a word. Otherwise, the letter is usually omitted. The English word *cart* was 'corrupted' *kyaat* in Jamaican Creole. The words *respect* and *car*, although 'corrupted', became *rispek* and *kyaar*, for example. This is not always the case, however. A notable exception to this is the Jamaican Creole word *wûrl* (pronounced like E. *world* without the *d*), which is used alongside *wol* (here the rule applies) and whose English equivalent is also *world*.

In most cases, a long 'a' sound (pronounced like 'a' in *path*) substitutes for 'ar' and the short 'or' sound occurring between two consonants. Examples include *kyaapet, shaap, maak, paak, faak,* and *laad* (E. *carpet, sharp, mark, park, fork,* and *lord*).

When 'er', 'or', 'ar', 'ur', and 'ure' occur at the end of a word, they are frequently replaced by a sharp 'a'. Examples include *waata, directa, pilla, solfa,* and *pikcha* (E. *water, director, pillar, sulfur,* and *picture*).

When 'd' and 'r' occur together, the combination is often pronounced like 'j'. Examples are *jap, jaiva,* and *jaah* (E. *drop, driver,* and *draw*).

When Consonants Occur Together

When two consonants occur together within or at the end of a word, there is a tendency to omit one of these letters (or to replace both with another letter in a small number of cases). Some examples are *tugedda, wol, wid,* and *aat* (E. *together, world, with,* and *art*).

'D' is frequently omitted when it occurs after 'n' or 'l' at the end of a word. Examples include *an, dimaan, ben, guol, kuol,* and *buol* (E. *and, demand, bend, gold, cold,* and *bold*).

In such cases where 's' occurs before 'm' in an English word, a vowel ('u' or, to a lesser extent, 'i') is frequently inserted between the two letters. Examples are *sumaal* and *sumuok* (E. *small* and *smoke*). When 's' occurs before 'n', an 'i' is frequently inserted between them. An example of this is *siniiz* (E. *sneeze*). 'S' is occasionally omitted before 't' and 'p' at the beginning of a word. Examples are *tan-op* and *pwuail* (E. *stand up* and *spoil*).

Long 'O' Sound

When the long English 'o' sound (even when represented by 'ou' and 'oa') occurs between two consonants, it is frequently substituted by 'uo'. Examples include *guol, kuot, buot,* and *suoda* (E. *gold, court, boat,* and *soda*).

'A' Sound

When the long English 'a' (pronounced like the *a* in gate) occurs between two consonants, it is frequently substituted by 'ye'. Examples are *lyet, gyet,* and *kyer* (E. *late, gate,* and *care*). When the sharp English 'a' (pronounced like *a* in car) occurs after 'c' or 'k' and before another consonant, it is frequently substituted by 'ya' when the word has one syllable and 'yaa' when the word has more than one syllable. Examples are *kyaar, kyaad,* and *kyabij* (E. *car, card,* and *cabbage*).

'B' Replaces 'V'

For emphasis, 'b' is sometimes used to replace 'v'. Some examples are *riba, ebriweh,* and *ebridyeh* (E. *river, everywhere,* and *everyday*).

Omitting And Adding 'H'

Some Jamaicans omit the *h* at the beginning of some words, for example, pronouncing *head* as *ed* and adding an *h* to words beginning with a vowel. Some Jamaicans pronounce *all* as *hall*. "W" is sometimes omitted or replaced with an 'h' before the 'u' sound at the beginning of a word (even when represented by 'oo' or 'ou'). For example, when 'h' is omitted E. *wood, would,* and *woman* become *ud, ud,* and *uhman.* When an 'h' replaces 'w', they become *hud, hud,* and *huhman,* respectively.

When Kk'l, K'l, Gg'l, And G'l Replace Ttl, Tl, Ddl, And Dl

'Ttl' and 'tl' are sometimes replaced by 'kk'l' and 'k'l', respectively. Examples are *likk'l* and *jengk'l* (E. *little* and *gentle*). 'Ddl' and 'dl' are sometimes replaced by 'gg'l' and 'g'l', respectively. Examples include *kyang'l* and *figg'l* (E. *candle* and *fiddle*).

Plural Of Yuh

There is both a singular and plural form of the word *yuh* (E. *you*) in Jamaican Creole, unlike in English where the word *you* is used to refer to both singular and plural subjects. The singular form is *yuh*, while the plural form is *unnu*. For example:

Sing.:	**Yuh a iih sista.**	You are his sister.
Plur.:	**Unnu run every dyeh.**	You run every day.

The Article Di

In Jamaican Creole, the definite article *di* (E. *the*) is usually omitted when mentioning non-specific nouns. The English language does this inconsistently, but Jamaican Creole consistently retains this rule. For example:

Jamaican Creole	*English*
Wi goh a <u>mall</u>.	We go to <u>the mall</u>.
Shi goh a <u>church</u>.	She goes to <u>church</u>.
Yuh goh a <u>club</u>.	You go to <u>the club</u>.

Build Your Jamaican Creole Vocabulary:

agoh *adv.* ago	**dem** *adj., pron.* their; them; they
di *adj., adv.* the	**pikni/pikini** *n.* child
mi *pron.* I; me	**wi** *adj., modal aux., pron.* our; we; us
uhman *n.* woman	

PRACTICE EXERCISE 1

Test the skills you have just learned by pronouncing the following words. You could also try to figure out the English equivalent:

baaba   faatnait   bredda   fishaman

kyaapet   madda   wi   granmadda

nevyu   wok   waa   haat

Lesson Two

Jamaican Creole Grammar

Sentences in Jamaican Creole generally have a subject, a verb, and a predicate. This is not always the case, however, because in some instances verbs are totally omitted from the sentence. Tenses in Jamaican Creole are, for the most part, consistent and simple. The challenge is mainly with sentence structure, which may vary depending on context.

The Simple Present Tense

In English, the simple present tense of a verb is conjugated based on the quantity of the subject as well as the person it refers to. Examples include *I run*, *She runs*, and *They run*. These conjugations do not exist in the simple present tense of Jamaican Creole, as verbs are not conjugated. In other words, the same base infinitive form of the verb is used for all subjects of the verb, whether singular or plural (the only exception is the verb *bi*, which will be dealt with shortly). Here are some examples of the simple present tense:

Jamaican Creole	English
Mi <u>drink</u> suoda.	I <u>drink</u> soda.
Iih <u>drink</u> suoda tuh.	He <u>drinks</u> soda too.
All a wi <u>drink</u> suoda.	All of us <u>drink</u> soda.
Dem <u>drink</u> suoda wid wi.	They <u>drink</u> soda with us.

As you can see in the examples above, the verb *drink* remains unchanged in its base infinitive form whether or not the subject is singular or plural. It can be reasoned that once the subject has been mentioned, it is easily understood who is drinking.

Build Your Jamaican Creole Vocabulary:

aada *n., v.* order

ajos *v.* adjust

bifuo *adv., conj., prep.* before

doppi *n.* ghost

eniweh *adv., pron.* anywhere

faak *n., v.* fork

gaaliin *n.* egret

iyego *n.* hypothermia

PRACTICE EXERCISE 2

Now that you have mastered the simple present tense, try to translate the following sentences to Jamaican Creole.

1. I like you.
2. You look nice today.
3. My brother owns a nice car.
4. Taylor says she likes John.
5. They present themselves well.
6. The apple falls from the tree.
7. The boys go to school.
8. The egret flies over the river.
9. She speaks French.
10. My mother works at the hospital.

Try to translate the following simple sentences to English.

1. Mi like di tyes a ackee.
2. Iih goh a di gym every dyeh.
3. Yuh always iht di syem ting pau Sunday.
4. Mi granmadda love church.
5. Di cat run afta di mus-mus.
6. Di likk'l bwuay jump pan di bed.
7. Shi have wau good vais.
8. Iih duh well inna school.
9. Mi anti love yam.
10. Deeh study inna di laibri.

Lesson Three

Present Conjugation Of The Verb Bi

The verb *bi* (E. *be*) is the only irregular verb in the simple present tense. It is conjugated *a*. It would therefore follow that *mi* (E. *I*), *iih, shi, ih* (E. *he, she, it*), and *yuh, dem, wi* (E. *you, they, we*) are all conjugated the same way. For example:

Jamaican Creole	*English*
Yuh <u>a</u> iih fren.	You <u>are</u> his friend.
Im <u>a</u> mi bes fren.	He <u>is</u> my best friend.
Di man <u>a</u> Jamaican.	The man <u>is</u> Jamaican.

When The Verb Bi Is Used Before Prepositions And Adverbs

The verb is irregular when used immediately before prepositions such as *a* (E. *at*), *pau* (E. *on*), *pan* (E. *on*), *inna* (E. *in*), *oova* (E, *over*), *anda* (E. *under*), etc., adverbs such as *ya* (E. *here*), *deh* (E. *there*), *dyer* (E. *there*), etc., that indicate location or position and becomes *deh* when used before them. In most instances, the sentence is usually indicating the physical location or position of the subject. For example:

11

Jamaican Creole	English
Mi <u>deh a</u> wok.	I <u>am at</u> work.
Dem <u>deh inna</u> di store.	They <u>are in</u> the store.
Im <u>deh anda</u> di bridge.	He <u>is under</u> the bridge.
Di blouse <u>deh pau</u> syel.	The blouse <u>is on</u> sale.

Despite this general rule, however, it is not uncommon for speakers of Jamaican Creole to totally dispose of the verb before prepositions such as *inna* (E. *in*), *oova* (E. *over*), *anda* (E. *under*), *dong* (E. *down*), *agens* (E. *against*), *afta* (E. *after*), and *aaf* (E. *off*). For example:

Jamaican Creole	English
Iih <u>inna</u> di house.	He <u>is in</u> the house.
Di bag <u>oova</u> deh.	The bag <u>is over</u> there.
Shi <u>dong</u> a di battam.	She <u>is down</u> at the bottom.

When The Verb Bi Is Used With Adjectives

The verb *bi* is irregular when used with adjectives. In such cases where the verb would occur immediately before an adjective, the verb is omitted. For example:

Jamaican Creole	English
Mi <u>sick</u>.	I <u>am sick</u>.
Di pikini <u>happy</u>.	The child <u>is happy</u>.
Di byebi <u>taiyad</u>.	The baby <u>is tired</u>.

Note that if an adverb occurs between the verb *bi* and the adjective, the above rule still stands. For example:

Jamaican Creole	English
Mi **buon** <u>taiyad</u>.	I <u>am</u> **bone** <u>tired</u>.
Shi **raada** <u>happy</u>.	She <u>is</u> **rather** <u>happy</u>.
Dem **really** <u>sick</u>.	They <u>are</u> **really** <u>sick</u>.

When an adjective indicates nationality, the conjugated form *a* is usually used. The verb can also be omitted. For example:

Jamaican Creole	English
Margarita <u>a</u> Cuban.	Margarita <u>is</u> Cuban.
Shi Jamaican.	She <u>is</u> Jamaican.
Mark Antiguan.	Mark <u>is</u> Antiguan.

When The Verb Bi Occurs At The End Of A Sentence

The verb *bi* is irregular when it occurs at the end of a sentence. Sentences are rarely constructed in this format, however. In this case, the verb is used in its base infinitive form, *bi*. For example:

Jamaican Creole	English
Deeh mek ih muo dan ih <u>bi</u>.	They make it more than it <u>is</u>.
Who nuo wa deeh <u>bi</u>.	Who knows what they <u>are</u>.
Dat a weh shi <u>bi</u>.	That is what she <u>is</u>.

When Ih Occurs Before And After A Or Words Beginning And Ending In The Letter A

Note that when *ih* (E. *it*) would occur immediately before the regular conjugated form of the verb *bi* (conjugated *a*), *ih* is usually omitted, or the English equivalent *it* is used instead. Where *ih* would **precede** a word beginning with the letter *a*, this rule also applies. When *ih* occurs **after** the regular form of the conjugated verb or follows a word ending with the letter *a*, E. *it* is always used. For example:

Jamaican Creole	*English*
<u>It a</u> di syem.	<u>It is</u> the same.
<u>A</u> fimmi.	<u>It is</u> mine.
Dat <u>a it</u>.	That <u>is it</u>.

This is probably because of how uncomfortable *ih* is to pronounce before or after *a*, or before or after words beginning or ending with *a*. Try it: *Ih a di syem.*

Build Your Jamaican Creole Vocabulary:

aaf *adj. adv., n., prep.* off

blakkin *n.* hibiscus

chring *n., v.* string

duo-wyeh *n.* doorway

jinal *n.* trickster

maaga *adj.* skinny

niiv'n *adv. phrase* not even

ops *adj.* meddlesome

PRACTICE EXERCISE 3

Translate the following sentences to Jamaican Creole, and determine whether to use *a*, *deh*, or *bi*.

1. I am at school.
2. We are in Spalding now.
3. The man is the mayor of Clarendon.
4. They are on the field.
5. The money is on the table.
6. The libraries are too far away.
7. That is what they say it is.
8. The director is in the boardroom.
9. His picture is on the wall.
10. The pillows are on the bed.

Indicate whether the following sentences make sense as they stand.

1. Aalduo Patsy deh a wok tudeh, shi still sick.
2. Shi a lonely.
3. Bob like di principal, an iih happy wid di wok weh iih duh inna di school.
4. Di daag a happy because im wag im tyel.
5. Ih a dotti.
6. Shi a di bes pilot.
7. Di bwuay sad bikaah im fyel im exam.
8. Wi a di few weh deh ya.
9. Ih daak.
10. Shi Japanese.

Lesson Four

The Present Continuous Tense

An example of the present continuous tense in English is *am studying*. In Jamaican Creole, it is formed by using the present tense of the verb *bi* (which is *a*) and the base infinitive form of the main verb. For example:

Jamaican Creole	*English*
Mi <u>a goh</u> a school.	I <u>am going</u> to school.
Shi <u>a spen</u> time ya.	She <u>is spending</u> time here.
Dem <u>a laugh</u>.	They <u>are laughing</u>.

In parts of Jamaica (such as the parish of St. Ann), the present tense of the verb *bi* is conjugated *deh* when used in the present continuous tense. So for the above examples, one would say:

Jamaican Creole	*English*
Mi <u>deh goh</u> a school.	I <u>am going</u> to school.
Shi <u>deh spen</u> time ya.	She <u>is spending</u> time here.
Dem <u>deh laugh</u>.	They <u>are laughing</u>.

Describing Multiple Actions

If more than one action or event are occurring at the same time, it is not necessary to repeat *a* or *deh* in the verb phrase to form the present continuous tense (this form can also be used, however). For example:

Jamaican Creole	*English*
Di pikni <u>a run an a jump</u>.	The child <u>is running and jumping</u>.
Wi <u>a huop an pryeh</u>.	We <u>are hoping and praying</u>.
Yuh <u>a listen an andastan</u>.	You <u>are listening and understanding</u>.

Less frequently, a form of the English present continuous tense is used in Jamaican Creole. The verb *be* that is used in English is omitted in Jamaican Creole, and the English present participle of the main verb ending in *-ing* is used. For example:

Jamaican Creole	*English*
Mi <u>going</u> to school.	I <u>am going</u> to school.
Shi <u>spending</u> time ya.	She <u>is spending</u> time here.
Dem <u>laughing</u>.	They <u>are laughing</u>.

Irregular Verbs Sidong And Tan-Op

The verbs *sidong* (E. *sit*) and *tan-op* (E. *stand*) are exceptions to the regular conjugation of verbs in the present continuous tense. These verbs are conjugated like the simple present tense. Therefore, if one wanted to say *They are sitting over there* or *They are standing over there*, one would say *Deeh sidong oova dehsoh* or *Deeh tan-op oova dehsoh*. If one were to say *Im a tan-op oova dehsoh*, it would indicate that the speaker is inferring that the person will be standing in the stated place at some point in the future, or that the person should be in the stated position because that is where they belong (especially if *inno* is used at the end of the sentence emphatically).

17

(The future tense is addressed in Lesson Eleven).

Build Your Jamaican Creole Vocabulary:

a soh *v. phrase* that is how; that is what

badmain *adj., n.* envy; envious

chuo *n., v.* throw

gi *v.* give

juk *n., v.* prick

kyaar *n.* car

mowli *adj.* moldy

noweh *adv., n.* nowhere

PRACTICE EXERCISE 4

Translate the following sentences to Jamaican Creole.

1. We are doing the work.
2. You are going to Jamaica.
3. He is tired, but he is climbing the long hill.
4. We are going to the beach party.
5. The child is learning well but needs more practice.
6. The sun seems like it is standing still in the sky.
7. Although the weather is bad, we are going to the river.
8. My friend is coming over, but I am leaving soon.
9. We are having lunch at the new seafood restaurant.
10. It is raining a lot, but I like it.

Translate the following sentences to English.

1. Im a lef tudeh wid im madda an im faada.
2. John a goh weh tomorrow an a tek im pet.
3. Di byebi a sleep pan di bed.
4. Wi a study fi di tes.
5. Di man a muo di lawn an a cut dong di tree.
6. Di tree weh tan-op pan di riva bank a gruo.
7. Shi a move nex mont.
8. Mi ha wok fi duh inna di yaad, but it a get daak.
9. Di daag a baak afta di shadow a di tree.
10. Mi a goh a beach wid mi family.

Lesson Five

Pluralizing

As in English, the part of speech of the Jamaican Creole word determines how it is pluralized. The pluralization of adjectives (demonstrative and possessive), nouns, and pronouns (personal and demonstrative) is addressed in this lesson.

Pluralizing Indefinite Adjectives And Adjectives Of Quantity

Examples of indefinite adjectives include E. *few*, E. *some*, and E. *many*. Examples of adjectives of quantity include E. *ten*, E. *five*, and E. *one*. Indefinite adjectives and adjectives of quantity have no plural form in English and in Jamaican Creole. Most of the indefinite adjectives and adjectives of quantity that are used in English are also used in Jamaican Creole. For example:

Jamaican Creole	*English*
<u>Nof</u> people nuo.	<u>A lot</u> [of] people know.
<u>One</u> pikni deh ya.	<u>One</u> child is here.
<u>Ten</u> kyang'l a bon.	<u>Ten</u> candles are burning.

Pluralizing Demonstrative Adjectives

The demonstrative adjectives in English are *this* and *that*. In Jamaican Creole, they include *da, dis, disya, dat,* and *datdeh*. They are pluralized as follows:

Singular	English	Plural	English
da/dis/disya	this	demya	these
da/dat/datdeh	that	demdeh	those

(The uses of da, dat, and datdeh are discussed in Lesson Twenty-One).

Examples Of Demonstrative Adjectives:

Jamaican Creole	English
<u>Demya</u> blouse ha huol inna dem.	<u>These</u> blouses have holes in them.
Wi a move <u>demdeh</u> tings out a di wyeh.	We are moving <u>those</u> things out of the way.
<u>Demya</u> bowl belong pan di shelf.	<u>These</u> bowls belong on the shelf.

Deh (E. *there*), *dyer* (E. *there*), and *ya* (E. *here*) are inserted after *da* to differentiate between *that* and *this. Dehsoh* (E. *there, right there*), *dyersoh* (E. *there, right there*), and *yasso* (E. *here, right here*) are also used to a lesser extent. *Deh, dyer, dehsoh,* and *dyersoh* are used with *da* to mean *that. Ya* and *yasso* are used with *da* to mean *this.* For example:

Jamaican Creole	English
<u>Da</u> blouse <u>ya</u> ha huol inna it.	<u>This</u> blouse <u>here</u> has holes in it.
Wi a move <u>da</u> ting <u>deh</u> out a di wyeh.	We are moving <u>that</u> thing <u>there</u> out of the way.
<u>Da</u> bowl <u>yasso</u> belong pan di shelf.	<u>This</u> bowl <u>right here</u> belongs on the shelf.

Deh (E. *there*), *dyer* (E. *there*), and *ya* (E. *here*) are sometimes inserted after a noun for emphasis or to indicate a specific location when used in conjunction with *disya*, *datdeh*, *demya*, and *demdeh*. *Dehsoh* (E. *there, right there*), *dyersoh* (E. *there, right there*), and *yasso* (E. *here, right here*) are also used to a lesser extent. *Ya* and *yasso* indicate a place close to the subject and are used with *disya* and *demya*. *Deh*, *dyer*, *dehsoh*, and *dyersoh* indicate a place at a distance and are used with *datdeh* and *demdeh*. For example:

Jamaican Creole	English
<u>Demya</u> blouse <u>yasso</u> ha huol inna dem.	<u>These</u> blouses <u>right here</u> have holes in them.
*<u>Wi</u> tink bout <u>demdeh</u> tings <u>deh</u>.	We think about <u>those</u> things <u>there</u>.
Put <u>disya</u> one <u>ya</u> pan di shelf.	Put <u>this</u> one <u>here</u> on the shelf.

* When used in this way, *deh* does not connote a literal place. It is used for emphasis in this example. *Dehsoh* and *dyersoh* always connote a literal place.

In some instances, *disya*, *datdeh*, *demya*, and *demdeh* are abbreviated *dis*, *dat*, *dem*, and *dem* when *deh*, *dyer*, *dehsoh*, *dyersoh*, *ya*, and *yasso* are inserted after the noun. This does not change the meaning of the sentence. For example:

Jamaican Creole	English
<u>Dem</u> blouse <u>dehsoh</u> ha huol inna dem.	<u>Those</u> blouses <u>right there</u> have holes in them.
Wi tink bout <u>dem</u> tings <u>deh</u>.	We think about <u>those</u> things <u>there</u>.
Put <u>dis</u> one <u>ya</u> pan di shelf.	Put <u>this</u> one <u>here</u> on the shelf.

Pluralizing Adjectives Demonstrating Possession

Table 1: Possessive Adjectives

Person	Singular	English	Plural	English
First	mi/fimmi	my	wi/fiwi	our
Second	yuh/fiyuh	your	unnu/fiunnu/fuunu	your
Third	iih/im/fihim	his	deeh/dem/fidem	their
Third	aar/fiar	her	deeh/dem/fidem	their
Third	ih/fiit/fihit	its	deeh/dem/fidem	their

(Adjectives demonstrating possession will be further discussed in Lesson Sixteen).

Pluralizing Nouns

Instead of adding 's' or 'es' to make nouns plural as is done in English, *dem* (E. *them*) is placed after the noun to make it plural. This is a condition only for nouns preceded by *di* (E. *the*), a noun demonstrating possession, or an adjective demonstrating possession. For example:

Jamaican Creole	English
<u>Di faama dem</u> deh a grong.	<u>The farmers</u> are at the field.
*<u>John house dem</u> deh pau syel.	<u>John's houses</u> are on sale.
*<u>Aar kyaar dem</u> run good.	<u>Her cars</u> run good/well.

*(Showing ownership is discussed in Lesson Sixteen).

Noun phrases that include an adjective that suggests that the noun is plural do not require *dem* to form their plural. Examples are *nof, muo,* and *five* (E. *a lot, more,* and *five*). The plural adjective automatically makes the noun phrase plural. This makes using *dem* redundant. For example:

Jamaican Creole	English
Nof uhman seh dem dislike di liida.	Plenty women say they dislike the leader.
Five mango inna di baaskit.	Five mangoes are in the basket.
Demdeh byebi deh cry all di time.	Those babies cry all the time.

It should be noted that general categories of nouns that do not fall into any of the preceding categories are not pluralized:

Jamaican Creole	English
Mi like daag an cat.	I like dogs and cats.
Daag like cat.	Dogs like cats.
Funeral sad muos time.	Funerals are sad most times.

There are a few exceptions to the above rule, however, with words like *iyer* and *ting* being pluralized *iyers* (E. *years*) and *tings* (E. *things*), except when preceded by *di* (E. *the*), a noun demonstrating possession, or an adjective demonstrating possession. In these cases, *dem* is used in addition to the plural form of each word. An example is *Tings deh ya* (E. *Things are here*) as opposed to *Di tings dem deh ya* (E. The *things are here*).

Certain plural nouns that are irregular in English, such as *people*, *furniture*, and *fish*, are used as they are in English and are not pluralized by adding *dem* unless they are preceded by *di*, a noun demonstrating possession, or an adjective demonstrating possession. Consider the following examples: *People love mi* (E. *People love me*) as opposed to *Di people dem a come* (E. *The people are coming*). Similarly, nouns that mainly occur in the plural form, such as *shoes*, *pants*, etc., are used as they are in English except when preceded by *di*, a noun demonstrating possession, or an adjective demonstrating possession.

A noun that follows a plural pronoun or a noun that has already been pluralized by adding *dem* is not pluralized. The noun is either used as it is, or an adjective that indicates the amount of the noun (e.g. *nof* (E. *plenty*)) is added. For example:

Jamaican Creole	English
Dem a fren.	They are friends.
*Di pikni dem ha dalli.	The children have dolls.
Di pikni dem ha two dalli.	The children have two dolls.

*It can be assumed that the specific number of dolls that the children have is not important to the speaker. If it were, the speaker would have explicitly stated the number.

Note, even if a noun or noun phrase has been pluralized with *dem*, if the second noun or noun phrase is preceded by *di* (E. *the*), a noun demonstrating possession, or adjective demonstrating possession, the second noun is usually made plural by adding *dem*. For example:

Jamaican Creole	English
Di tiif dem tiif di kyaar dem an di book dem.	The thieves stole the cars and the books.
*Mi fren dem gi fidem pikni dem mango.	My friends give their children mangoes.
Di employee dem like all a di building dem weh dem wok inna.	The employees like all of the buildings that they work in.

*Note in the second example that *mango* is not pluralized in Jamaican Creole. This is because *mangoes* are a general category of nouns, and the mangoes mentioned are referred to in a nonspecific way. Had *mango* been preceded by *di*, a noun demonstrating possession, or an adjective demonstrating possession, *dem* would be added to pluralize the noun. For example, the sentence would be *Mi fren dem gi fidem pikni dem di mango dem* (E. *My friends give their children the mangoes*) or *Mi fren dem gi fidem pikni dem fidem mango dem* (E. *My friends give their children their mangoes*).

If it needs to be made known that a group of people falls into the same category or that a person is somehow associated with one or a few individuals familiar to the speaker and hearer, then this is communicated by mentioning the name of that person or those few persons and adding *dem*. For example:

Jamaican Creole	English
<u>Sasha dem</u> a pyent di house.	<u>Sasha [and company]</u> are painting the house.
<u>James an Patricia dem</u> a come.	James and <u>Patricia [and company]</u> are coming.
Mi nuo <u>Harris dem</u>.	I know <u>Harris [and company]</u>.

Pluralizing Personal Pronouns

Personal pronouns are pluralized as follows:

Table 2: Subject Personal Pronouns

Singular	English	Plural	English
mi	I	wi	we
yuh	you	unnu	you
iih/im	he	dem/deeh	they
shi	she	dem/deeh	they
ih/E. it	it	dem/deeh	they

Table 3: Object Personal Pronouns

Singular	English	Plural	English
mi	me	wi	us
yuh	you	unnu	you
im/E. him	him	dem	them
*aar/E. she	her	dem	them
ih/E. it	it	dem	them

*E. *She* is frequently used instead of *aar* following the regular present conjugation of the verb *bi*, e.g., *A she* (E. *It is she*).

Table 4: Possessive Personal Pronouns

Singular	English	Plural	English
fimmi	mine	fiwi	ours
fiyuh	yours	fuunu/fiunnu	yours
fihim	his	fidem	theirs
fiar	hers	fidem	theirs
fiit/fihit	its	fidem	theirs

(The use of possessive pronouns is discussed in Lesson Sixteen).

Table 5: Reflexive Personal Pronouns

Singular	English	Plural	English
miself	myself	wiself	ourselves
yuhself	yourself	unnuself	yourselves
iihself/ imself	himself	deehself/demself	themselves
aarself	herself	deehself/demself	themselves
ihself	itself	deehself/demself	themselves

The above pronouns are used in similar contexts as they are in English. For example:

Jamaican Creole	English
<u>Deeh</u> like fish.	<u>They</u> like fish.
<u>Wi</u> duh evriting <u>wiself</u>.	<u>We</u> do everything <u>ourselves</u>.
<u>Unnu</u> a di bes.	<u>You</u> are the best.
Tell <u>dem</u>.	Tell <u>them</u>.

Pluralizing Demonstrative Pronouns

The demonstrative pronouns in English are *this* and *that*. In Jamaican Creole, they include *dis, disya, dat*, and *datdeh*. They are pluralized as follows:

Singular	English	Plural	English
dis/disya	this	demya	these
dat/datdeh	that	demdeh	those

Some examples of demonstrative pronouns include:

Jamaican Creole	English
<u>Demya</u> blue.	<u>These</u> are blue.
Mi wau <u>disya</u>.	I want <u>this</u>.
<u>Demdeh</u> good.	<u>Those</u> are good.

Pluralizing Indefinite Pronouns

Examples of indefinite pronouns include E. *some*, E. *much*, and E. *few*. These words have no plural form in English and in Jamaican Creole. Most of the indefinite pronouns that are used in English are also used in Jamaican Creole. For example:

Jamaican Creole	English
Mi wau <u>nof</u>.	I want <u>a lot</u>.
Im give im <u>all</u>.	He gives his <u>all</u>.
<u>Some</u> nuo wi.	<u>Some</u> know us.

Build Your Jamaican Creole Vocabulary:

ayri *slang* ok; great

bagabu *n.* caterpillar

blinki *n.* firefly

chi-chi *n.* termite

saach *v.* search

tik *adj., adv., n., v.* stick; thick

wa *adj., adv., interj., pron.* what

ya *adv., n.* here

PRACTICE EXERCISE 5

Translate the following sentences to Jamaican Creole, and determine whether *dem* should be used to make the sentence plural.

1. The children are on the school bus.
2. The girls visit their grandmother almost every month.
3. Some dogs like bananas.
4. A lot of people work on the farm.
5. Some of the students of class one do well in Spanish class.
6. Six boys from the football team are also in the Tourism club.
7. Tina, Arnold, and the rest go to the same school.
8. My cousins plant bananas and yams on the farms.
9. They put up all the paintings and relics in the museum.
10. John likes all of his co-workers.

Indicate whether the following sentences make sense as they stand. Try to correct the incorrect sentences.

1. Nof people dem deh a di bus stop.
2. Di two man a suolja inna di Jamaica Defense Force.
3. Sooh new furniture store deh a Montego Bay.
4. Di rubbish truck service two town a di syem time every dyeh.
5. Nof tourist come a Jamaica inna Disemba.
6. Pamela like all aar fren, but shi prefa Dawn.
7. All a di shop cluoz pau Sunday.
8. Aalduo di tiicha like di student dem, shi put dem nyem pau di detention lis.
9. Five a di memba dem deh inna di club.
10. Fifty swim team enta di competition dis iyer.

Lesson Six

The Simple Past Tense

The simple past tense in Jamaican Creole is not construed in exactly the same way as the simple past tense in English. There are primarily five ways to state something so that it is understood to have occurred in the past. You learned in *Lesson Two* that the simple present tense is formed by using the base infinitive form of the verb for all subjects of the verb, whether singular or plural. This same principle applies to the simple past tense, except how far in the past the action occurred also has bearing on how it is related. It can be formed in the following ways:

i. In Jamaican Creole, actions that occurred in the distance past are thought of differently than are actions that occurred in the recent past (close to the present moment). *Did* (or less commonly *beeh, weeh, beeh did,* or *weeh did*) is placed before the base infinitive form of the verb to indicate that the action occurred at a distant time in the past. For example:

Jamaican Creole	*English*
Mi <u>did goh</u> a bank.	I <u>went</u> to the bank.
Deeh <u>beeh did tink</u> shi tall.	They <u>thought</u> she was tall.
Di two doctor dem <u>weeh meet</u> inna Kingston.	The two doctors <u>met</u> in Kingston.

When a sentence has two clauses (whether it is two independent clauses or an independent and a dependent clause), one verb is often used in the past tense to make the rest of the sentence past. The present form of the other verb/s is/are used, even if it is being communicated that a second action also took place in the past. If the sentence has a dependent and an independent clause, the verb mentioned in the independent clause is the one that is usually conjugated to the past tense. For example:

Jamaican Creole	*English*
Suzie <u>did feel</u> taiyad afta wok, soh shi goh a bed.	Suzie <u>felt</u> tired after work, so she went to bed.
Mi <u>weeh did goh</u> a di paati, auh mi sista goh a church.	I <u>went</u> to the party, and my sister went to church.
Di two paati dem <u>beeh mek</u> wau deal, soh dem sign di pyepa dem.	The two parties <u>made</u> a deal, so they signed the papers.

You should note that there is no harm done if you were to say:

> Mi <u>*did goh*</u> *a di paati, aalduo mi sista* <u>*did goh*</u> *a church* (E. *I* <u>went</u> *to the party, although my sister* <u>went</u> *to church*), or Mi <u>*did goh*</u> *a di paati, aalduo mi sista* <u>*goh*</u> *a church* (E. *I* <u>went</u> *to the party, although my sister* <u>went</u> *to church*).

Both sentences are grammatically correct.

2. If the time that the action took place is mentioned, the need to put *did, beeh, weeh, beeh did*, or *weeh did* before the verb to form its past tense is optional. For example:

Jamaican Creole	English
Yessideh, wi <u>iht</u> a di restaurant.	Yesterday, we <u>ate</u> at the restaurant.
Two dyeh agoh, wi <u>goh</u> a riva.	Two days ago, we <u>went</u> to the river.
Wedyeh, mi anti <u>come</u> a mi house.	The other day, my aunt <u>came</u> to my house.

Note, however, that it is not incorrect to use *did* to form the past tense of a verb even if the time at which the event took place in the past is mentioned. An example is *Yessideh, wi <u>did iht</u> a di restaurant* (E. *Yesterday, we <u>ate</u> at the restaurant*).

3. When conversing in Jamaican Creole and it has previously been established that the events being discussed took place at a time in the past, the present tense is frequently used to relate the rest of the idea or story. For example, if you asked someone what they did yesterday and they were in school, they might respond:

Jamaican Creole

Mi <u>did deh</u> a school. Di tiicha <u>teach</u> wau new topic. Shi <u>talk</u> bout di Taino dem auh di wyeh dem <u>faam</u>. Shi <u>seh</u> wi fi <u>research</u> di topic muo auh <u>come</u> back wid wau shaat essay.

English

I <u>was</u> at school. The teacher <u>taught</u> a new topic. She <u>talked</u> about the Tainos and the way they <u>farmed</u>. She <u>said</u> we <u>should research</u> the topic more and <u>come</u> back with a short essay.

4. When an action began in the past but has implications for the present, the simple present tense is frequently used (although this is usually when the event or action occurred in the recent past). For example:

Jamaican Creole	English
Deeh <u>styeshan</u> im a Spalding.	They <u>stationed</u> him in Spalding.
Patrick <u>fix</u> di pipe, but it a leak.	Patrick <u>fixed</u> the pipe, but it is leaking.
Iih <u>iht</u> di food an <u>lef</u> di plyet pan di tyeb'l.	He <u>ate</u> the food and <u>left</u> the plate on the table.

5. If an action or event recently took place, such as immediately before it was related, the simple present tense is frequently used to relate the event or action. For example:

Jamaican Creole	English
Bess <u>chuo-weh</u> di milk pan di floor.	Bess <u>spilled</u> the milk onto the floor.
Iih <u>look</u> pau yuh funny.	He <u>looked</u> at you funny.
Sheldon <u>tek</u> ih out a iih pakit.	Sheldon <u>took</u> it out of his pocket.

Build Your Jamaican Creole Vocabulary:

aal now *adv. phrase* even now

bandulu *adj.* illegal

dehsoh *adv., n.* there

fi *prep., mod. aux.* for; should; ought to; to

kip *v.* keep

magij *n.* maggot

nomo *adv.* no more; any longer

ol *adj.* old

PRACTICE EXERCISE 6

Translate the following sentences to Jamaican Creole. Try to use all the forms of the past tense that you learned.

1. Many people came after the show started.
2. We got to the airport on time.
3. When I looked up at the sky, the clouds looked dark.
4. He disliked the teacher.
5. The grass looked green two weeks ago, but now it is brown.
6. Rain fell yesterday, and I hope it falls again today.
7. The car crashed into a pole at the side of the road.
8. Two days ago, Sally worked on the night shift.
9. When I lived in Toronto, I worked as a nurse.
10. The dog barked at the noisy truck.

The following sentences should be in the simple past tense. Correct the ones that are incorrect, and try rewriting each sentence in the five forms of the simple past tense that you learned. Remember that context needs to be taken into account with the simple past tense. Try to imagine that the event or action took place some time in the past (recent or farther), and you are relating it to another person.

1. Mi iht inna di iivlin, soh mi full.
2. Wi did lie dong pan di beach while ryen a fall, an mi ketch kuol.
3. Shi lef yessideh.
4. Di winda beeh did opin, an di ryen wet di bed.
5. Dem plyeh pan di team when mi faada goh a high school.
6. Jos now, iih pyent di wall.
7. Mi tink iih nuo seh ih wrong when iih did dwiit.
8. Di byebi did cry when iih madda did lef.
9. Shi weeh blyem im fi fyel aar exam dem.
10. Iih get five dalla fi goh a school dis maanin.

Lesson Seven

The Case Of The Verb Bi In The Simple Past Tense

The verb *bi* (E. *be*) is irregular in the simple past tense. It is conjugated *did a* (or less commonly *ben a*, *wen a*, *beeh did a*, or *weeh did a*). It would therefore follow that *mi* (E. *I*), *iih, shi, ih* (E. *he, she, it*), and *yuh, dem, wi* (E. *you, they, we*) are all conjugated the same way, which is *did a* (*ben a, wen a, beeh did a,* or *weeh did a*). For example:

Jamaican Creole	*English*
Yuh <u>did a</u> iih fren.	You <u>were</u> his friend.
Im <u>beeh did a</u> di bes tiicha mi ha.	He <u>was</u> the best teacher I had.
Di man <u>wen a</u> Jamaican.	The man <u>was</u> Jamaican.

Reversing Did A

When using *did a* (but **not** *ben a, wen a, beeh did a,* or *weeh did a*), the format of the verb can be reversed. So, we can use *a did* where we would use *did a*. For example:

Jamaican Creole	English
Yuh <u>a did</u> iih fren.	You <u>were</u> his friend.
Im <u>a did</u> di bes tiicha mi ha.	He <u>was</u> the best teacher I had.
Di man <u>a did</u> Jamaican.	The man <u>was</u> Jamaican.

When The Verb Bi Is Used Before Prepositions And Adverbs

The verb *bi* is irregular when used directly before prepositions such as *a* (E. *at*), *pan* (E. *on*), *pau* (E. *on*), *inna* (E. *in*), *oova* (E, *over*), *anda* (E. *under*), *dong* (E. *down*), etc., and adverbs such as *ya* (E. *here*), *deh* (E. *there*), *dyer* (E. *there*), etc., that indicate position or location and becomes *did deh* (or less commonly *beeh deh, weeh deh, beeh did deh,* or *weeh did deh*) when used before them. In most instances, the sentence is usually indicating the physical location or position of the subject. For example:

Jamaican Creole	English
Di blouse <u>did deh pau</u> syel.	The blouse <u>was on</u> sale.
Wi <u>beeh did deh dong</u> by di seaside.	We <u>were down</u> by the seaside.
Im <u>did deh oova</u> dyer.	He <u>was over</u> there.
Di jam <u>weeh deh inna</u> di fridge.	The jam <u>was in</u> the fridge.

Despite this general rule, however, it is not uncommon for speakers of Jamaican Creole to shorten the verb, disposing of *deh* before prepositions such as *inna* (E. *in*), *oova* (E. *over*), *anda* (E. *under*), *dong* (E. *down*), *agens* (E. *against*), *afta* (E. *after*), and *aaf* (E. *off*). *Did, beeh, weeh, beeh did,* and *weeh did* are retained before the previously mentioned prepositions. For example:

Jamaican Creole	English
Iih <u>did inna</u> di house.	He <u>was in</u> the house.
Di bag <u>beeh did oova</u> dyer.	The bag <u>was over</u> there.
Dem <u>did dong</u> a di battam.	They <u>were down</u> at the bottom.
Wi <u>weeh aaf</u> di committee.	We <u>were off</u> the committee.

Note that *deh* should **not** be disposed of before these prepositions and adverbs: *a, pan, pau, deh, dyer,* and *ya.* For example:

Jamaican Creole	English
Mi <u>did deh a</u> wok when ih ha'mn.	I <u>was at</u> work when it happened.
Di kyek <u>beeh deh pan</u> di tyeb'l.	The cake <u>was on</u> the table.
Im <u>weeh did deh ya.</u>	He <u>was here.</u>

When The Verb Bi Is Used With Adjectives

When used before an adjective (for example, *happy, sad,* or *pretty*), the verb is abbreviated *did* (or less commonly *beeh, weeh, beeh did,* or *weeh did*). For example:

Jamaican Creole	English
Mi <u>did sick.</u>	I <u>was sick.</u>
Aalduo wi did lose all a di money, wi <u>beeh did happy.</u>	Although we lost all of the money, we <u>were happy.</u>
Iih <u>weeh lonely,</u> soh iih get wau daag.	He <u>was lonely,</u> so he got a dog.

Note that if an adverb is placed between the verb *bi* and the adjective, the above rule still stands. For example:

Jamaican Creole	English
Mi <u>did **buon** taiyad</u>.	I <u>was **bone** tired</u>.
Shi <u>beeh did **raada** happy</u>.	She <u>was **rather** happy</u>.
Dem <u>weeh **really** sick</u>.	They <u>were **really** sick</u>.

The verb is irregular when it occurs at the end of a sentence. Sentences are rarely constructed in this format, however. In this case, the verb is conjugated *did bi* (or less commonly *beeh bi, weeh bi, beeh did bi,* or *weeh did bi*). For example:

Jamaican Creole	English
Deeh mek ih muo dan ih <u>did bi</u>.	They make it more than it <u>was</u>.
Who nuo wa deeh <u>beeh did bi</u>.	Who knows what they <u>were</u>.
Dat a weh shi <u>weeh bi</u>.	That is what she <u>was</u>.

Build Your Jamaican Creole Vocabulary:

anansi *n.* spider

baal *adj., n., v.* bald; cry; shave

kech *n., v.* catch; reach

mash *v.* shatter; to step on

quiz *n., v.* squeeze

san *n., v.* sand

tek *adj., n., v.* take; witty (slang)

PRACTICE EXERCISE 7

Translate the following sentences to Jamaican Creole.

1. They were the only ones there.
2. The river was deeper a year ago.
3. It was less than we thought it was.
4. The musicians were at a party.
5. That was the name of the book.
6. They were in the store when we passed.
7. It was on the table, but now it's gone.
8. The old woman was very sick.
9. It was his job.
10. Charlie was very sad when his sister went away.

Look at the following sentences, and try to determine if the sentences make sense as they stand.

1. Di bod beeh did deh inna di tree.
2. Wi did nuo weh ih a.
3. Pablo weeh happy seh iih pass di exam.
4. It a windy yessideh.
5. Di movie ben a scary.
6. Deeh did a di two bes musician dem inna di country.
7. Montego Bay did hat.
8. Mi granmadda did a mi bes fren.
9. Di pikni dem ben a a di paak.
10. Deeh did deh a di shuo.

Lesson Eight

The Continuous Past Tense

An example of the continuous past tense in English is *were having*. In Jamaica Creole, the continuous past tense is formed by using the past tense of the verb *bi*, which is *did a* (or less frequently *ben a, wen a, did deh, beeh deh, weeh deh, beeh did deh,* or *weeh did deh*), with the base infinitive form of the main verb. For example:

Jamaican Creole	*English*
Wi <u>did a sleep</u>.	We <u>were sleeping</u>.
Dem <u>beeh did deh pyent</u> di room.	They <u>were painting</u> the room.
Iih <u>wen a paati</u> laas night.	He <u>was partying</u> last night.

Irregular Verbs Sidong And Tan-Op

The verbs *sidong* (E. *sit*) and *tan-op* (E. *stand*) are exceptions to the regular conjugation of verbs in the continuous past tense. These verbs are conjugated like the simple past tense that utilizes *did, beeh, weeh, beeh did,* and *weeh did*. For example:

Jamaican Creole	*English*
Deeh <u>did sidong</u> oova dehsoh.	They <u>were sitting</u> over there.
Deeh <u>beeh tan-op</u> oova dehsoh.	They <u>were standing</u> over there.
John <u>weeh did tan-op</u> pan di varanda.	John <u>was standing</u> on the veranda.

Build Your Jamaican Creole Vocabulary:

aalduo *conj.* although

chigga *n.* jigger

dyersoh *adv., n.* there

grii *v. phrase* get along

ha *v.* have

kowl *adj., n.* cold

mek *v.* let; make; allow

tegreg/tegereg *n.* impolite or cantankerous person

PRACTICE EXERCISE 8

Translate the following sentences to Jamaican Creole.

1. They were dancing at the party last night.
2. David is behind in his work, so he was working last night.
3. She was ironing her clothes.
4. We were living in Port Royal when the earthquake shook.
5. We were eating dinner in the living room because the dining room was messy.
6. They were fighting with their fists.
7. The dog was sleeping on the mat at the front of the house.
8. They were hunting wild pigs in the woods.
9. The radio was playing on 107 FM.
10. It was getting late.

Translate the following sentences to English.

1. Ih did a get kuol.
2. Dem ben a get ready fi goh a church.
3. Di apple dem did deh jap aaf a di tree inna di backyaad.
4. Wi weeh did deh study fi di mathematics exam.
5. Iih did a get ready fi wok.
6. Di tiicha wen a pyes pyepa pan di wall.
7. Di pikni dem did a plyeh inna di yaad.
8. Di guot did deh iht grass out inna di grong.
9. Wi weeh deh watch television when di tiif brok chruu di winda.
10. Di meat tyes funny bikaah ih did a bon.

Lesson Nine

The Present Perfect Tense

Examples of the present perfect tense in English are *have given* and *is seen*. In Jamaican Creole, this tense is construed somewhat differently. Main verbs used with *ha* (E. *have*) are used differently than verbs used with *bi* (E. *be*). The verb *ha* is omitted, and the main verb is simply used in its base infinitive form in Jamaican Creole. There are indicators (usually adverbs), however, that suggest that the action is still taking place in the present, or that it has some implications for the present (e.g., *now, already*). For example:

Jamaican Creole	English
Deeh <u>drink</u> five beer areddi.	lit. They <u>drink</u> five beers already. (*They have drunk five beers already*).
Shi <u>lef</u> lang time agoh.	lit. She <u>leaves</u> [a] long time ago. (*She has left [a] long time ago*).
Deeh <u>siit</u> bifuo.	lit. They <u>see it</u> before. (*They have seen it before*).

The verb *bi* (E. *be*) is omitted since the past participle of the main verb acts like an adjective, and the verb is omitted before adjectives. For example:

Jamaican Creole	English
Ih <u>iht</u>.	lit. It <u>is eat</u>. (*It is eate*n).
Dem <u>sell</u> inna di store.	lit. They <u>sell</u> in the store. (*They are sold in the store*).
Shi <u>prepare</u>.	lit. She <u>prepare</u>. (*She is prepared*).

When The Verb Bi Is The Main Verb

In the present perfect tense, the speaker can choose to frame the sentence in either of two ways when *bi* is the main verb. These are discussed below:

Instance One

The verb can be conjugated like the present tense (review if necessary). An adverb or phrase indicating that the action took place in the past and continues to the present is necessary to convey meaning. For example:

Jamaican Creole	English
Shi <u>deh</u> ya frau yessideh.	lit. She <u>is</u> here from yesterday. (*She has been here from yesterday*).
Mi <u>a</u> di principal one iyer now.	lit. I <u>am</u> the principal one year now. (*I have been the principal one year now*).
Penny <u>a</u> mi fren since high school.	lit. Penny <u>is</u> my friend since high school. (*Penny has been my friend since high school*).

Instance Two

The verb can be conjugated like the English present perfect tense (E. *been*). The verb *have* that precedes the past participle of the main verb *be* in English is omitted in Jamaican Creole. For example:

45

Jamaican Creole	English
Mi <u>been</u> sick.	I [have] been sick.
Mi <u>been</u> dyer.	I [have] been there.
Wi <u>been</u> aroun.	We [have] been around.

Compound verbs such as *has been taken* are not used in Jamaican Creole. If one wanted to say, for example, *She has been taken to the hospital*, one could say *Dem tek aar to di hospital* (E. *They took her to the hospital*).

The Verb Goh In The Present Perfect Tense
The verb *goh* (E. *go*) is one of two irregular verbs in the present perfect tense. Its conjugation bears similarity to the English conjugation. The same past participle (E. *gone*) is used in Jamaican Creole, but the verbs *ha* and *bi* are omitted in Jamaican Creole. For example:

Jamaican Creole	English
Ih <u>gone</u>.	It [is] gone.
Dem <u>gone</u> huom.	They [have] gone home.
Shi <u>gone</u> a supamaakit.	She [has] gone to the supermarket.
Dem <u>gone</u>.	They [are] gone.

The Verb Duh In The Present Perfect Tense
The verb *duh* (E. *do*) is irregular in the present perfect tense when preceded by the verb *bi* (but not the verb *ha*). Its conjugation bears similarity to the English conjugation. The same past participle (E. *done*) is used in Jamaican Creole, but the verb *be* that would precede *done* in English is omitted in Jamaican Creole. For example:

Jamaican Creole	English
Mi <u>done</u>.	I [am] <u>done</u>.
Deeh <u>done</u> talk.	They [are] <u>done</u> talking.
Martha <u>done</u> wid ih.	Martha [is] <u>done</u> with it.

When *duh* is associated with the verb *ha*, the verb *duh* behaves like a regular verb and is conjugated as in the present tense. The verb *ha* is omitted in Jamaican Creole. For example:

Jamaican Creole	English
Mi <u>duh</u> it areddi.	lit. I <u>do</u> it already. (*I have done it already*).
Wi <u>duh</u> well inna di exam.	lit. We <u>do</u> well in the exam. (*We have done well in the exam*).
Iih <u>duh</u> iihself proud.	lit. He <u>does</u> himself proud. (*He has done himself proud*).

The Continuous Present Perfect Tense

An example of the continuous present perfect tense in English is *has been feeling*. In Jamaican Creole, the simple present tense or the continuous present tense is used in place of the continuous present perfect tense. When the simple present tense is used in place of the continuous present perfect tense, an indication is given about how long the action has been going on for, up until the present. For example:

Jamaican Creole:
   Mi <u>live</u> abroad fi <u>five iyers now</u>.

English:
   lit. I <u>live</u> abroad for <u>five years now</u>.
   (*I <u>have been living</u> abroad for <u>five years now</u>*).

In other cases where no indication is given about how long the action has been going on for, the continuous present tense is used. For example:

Jamaican Creole:
> Mi <u>a read</u> di book.

English:
> lit. I <u>am reading</u> the book.
> (*I <u>have been reading</u> the book*).

Less frequently, a form of the English continuous present perfect tense is used in Jamaican Creole. The verb *have* that is used in English is omitted in Jamaican Creole, and the English verb *be* along with the present participle of the main verb ending in *-ing* are used. For example:

Jamaican Creole:
> Im <u>been feeling</u> well.

English:
> He <u>has been feeling</u> well.

For the purpose of distinguishing between the English conjugation and the Jamaican Creole conjugation, -in is used instead of –ing for Jamaican Creole verbs (e.g., *duh-in* (E. *doing*)).

Build Your Jamaican Creole Vocabulary:

aweh *adv.* away

datdeh *adj., pron.* that

faam *n., v.* farm; form; pretend to be

indeh *contr.* in there

jangcro *n.* vulture

nyeli *adv.* nearly

ong'l *adj., adv.* only

yasso *adv., n.* here

PRACTICE EXERCISE 9

Translate the following sentences to Jamaican Creole. Use any adverb or adverb phrase that you think might help make the meaning of the sentence clearer.

1. They have worked at the library.
2. We have been saying that for years.
3. John has painted in the basement.
4. The teacher has been leaving class early.
5. The rain has been falling.
6. The dogs have played with the cat.
7. It has been taking a while.
8. The same movie has been playing for almost an hour now.
9. They have studied Swahili.
10. The woman has been going to the beach.

Lesson Ten

The Past Perfect Tense

Examples of the past perfect tense in English are *had held* and *was shown*. In Jamaican Creole, the past perfect tense is formed by using *did* (and to a lesser extent *beeh, weeh, beeh did*, or *weeh did*) along with the base infinitive form of the verb. This is one of the conjugations used in the simple past tense as discussed in *Lesson Six*. The following sentences are examples of the past perfect tense:

Jamaican Creole	*English*
Shi <u>did gi</u> mi di kyaar.	She <u>had given</u> me the car.
Iih <u>weeh sing</u> pan di kwaiya when iih likk'l.	He <u>had sung</u> on the choir when he was little.
Iih <u>beeh did put</u> ih pau wau tray pan di tyeb'l.	He <u>had put</u> it on a tray on the table.

The past perfect tense that is formed with the verb *be* in English is not used in Jamaican Creole. For example, instead of saying *She was seen by them*, one would say *Dem did si aar* (E. *They saw her*). This indicates a preference for the active, as opposed to the passive voice.

The Verb Bi In The Past Perfect Tense

In the past perfect tense, the verb *bi* (E. *be*) behaves as it does in the simple past tense (revise if necessary). For example:

Jamaican Creole	*English*
Paul <u>did deh</u> ya when ih ha'mn.	Paul <u>had been</u> here when it happened.
Di daag <u>beeh did</u> happy a di house.	The dog <u>had been</u> happy at the house.
Monica <u>wen a</u> di laas one fi lef.	Monica <u>had been</u> the last one to leave.

Compound verbs such as *had been taken* are not used in Jamaican Creole. If one wanted to say, for example, *She had been taken to the hospital*, one would say *Dem did tek aar to di hospital* (E. *They had taken her to the hospital*).

The Verb Goh In The Past Perfect Tense

In the past perfect tense, the regular conjugation of the verb *goh* (E. *go*) is *did goh* (or to a lesser extent *beeh goh, weeh goh, beeh did goh*, or *weeh did goh*). For example:

Jamaican Creole	*English*
Mi <u>did goh</u> a school.	I <u>had gone</u> to school.
Dem <u>weeh goh</u> huom.	They <u>had gone</u> home.
Shi <u>beeh goh</u> a supamaakit.	She <u>had gone</u> to the supermarket.

However, if one is relating that the action had happened while another event had been going on, or if both actions happened in close temporal proximity, the English participle *gone* is most often used along with *did* (or to a lesser extent *beeh, weeh, beeh did*, or *weeh did*). For example:

Jamaican Creole	English
Mi <u>did gone</u> a school when dem come.	I <u>had gone</u> to school when they came.
Dem <u>weeh gone</u> huom afta mi lef.	They <u>had gone</u> home after I left.
Shi <u>beeh did gone</u> a supamaakit when yuh call.	She <u>had gone</u> to the supermarket when you called.

The Continuous Past Perfect Tense

An example of the continuous past perfect tense in English is *had been playing*. In Jamaican Creole, the continuous past perfect tense is formed like the continuous past tense. *Did a* (and to a lesser extent *ben a, wen a, did deh, beeh deh, weeh deh, beeh did deh,* or *weeh did deh*) is used before the base infinitive form of the verb. For example:

Jamaican Creole	English
Iih <u>did a watch</u> TV.	He <u>had been watching</u> TV.
John <u>beeh did deh dance</u> salsa a di nightclub.	John <u>had been dancing</u> salsa at the nightclub.
Mi <u>weeh deh expek</u> fi lef wok early tudeh.	I <u>had been expecting</u> to leave work early today.

Build Your Jamaican Creole Vocabulary:

adda *adj., adv., pron.* other

baada *n., v.* border

hyeh *v.* hear

laba *v.* to talk excessively

red *adj.* drunk

si *v.* see

taiyadin *adj.* tiring

uolbrok *n.* secondhand clothes; anything secondhand

PRACTICE EXERCISE 10

Translate the following sentences to Jamaican Creole.

1. He had sold his car.
2. They had told her to ship the parcel.
3. The sky had been cloudy all day.
4. Although he is happy now, he had been sad last week.
5. The student had finished the assignment.
6. The ship had left the harbor one hour before it was scheduled to leave.
7. They had been studying at the library.
8. He had been doing his best.
9. The boy had been washing his clothes.
10. We had been cleaning the kitchen and painting the walls.

Lesson Eleven

The Future Tense

An example of the future tense in English is *will have*. In Jamaican Creole, it is formed in two ways:

1. By placing the auxiliary verb *a goh* (also used as *ooh* or *aggo*) before the base infinitive form of the main verb to indicate that the action or event is going to occur in the future. For example:

Jamaican Creole	*English*
Wi <u>aggo wok</u> pan di research.	We <u>are going to work</u> on the research.
Di man <u>a goh plyeh</u> pan di team.	The man <u>is going to play</u> on the team.
Mi <u>ooh buy</u> wau new bag.	I <u>am going to buy</u> a new bag.

2. By placing the auxiliary verb *gweeh* before the base infinitive form of the verb to mean *will* or *is/are going to*. For example:

Jamaican Creole	English
Iih <u>gweeh dwiit</u>.	He <u>will/is going to do it</u>.
Wi <u>gweeh iht</u> afta wi finish.	We <u>will/are going to eat</u> after we are finished.
Ih <u>gweeh ha'mn</u> agen.	It <u>will/is going to happen</u> again.

The Verb Bi In The Future Tense

In the future tense, the auxiliary verbs *a goh* (*ooh* or *aggo*) and *gweeh* are used before the base infinitive form of the verb *bi* to mean *will be*. For example:

Jamaican Creole	English
Wi <u>aggo bi</u> inna Christiana soon.	We <u>will be</u> in Christiana soon.
It <u>aggo bi</u> aarait.	It <u>will be</u> alright.
Sandy <u>gweeh bi</u> di fos uhman fi win di tournament.	Sandy <u>will be</u> the first woman to win the tournament.

It is not uncommon, however, for the main verb to be omitted and for *a goh* (*ooh* or *aggo*) or *gweeh* to be retained before adjectives. For example:

Jamaican Creole	English
Yuh <u>aggo sick</u>.	You <u>are going to be sick</u>.
Jim <u>gweeh happy</u>.	Jim <u>is going to be happy</u>.
Im <u>aggo glad</u> fiit.	He <u>will be glad</u> for it.

When an intervening adverb occurs between the conjugated verb or verb phrase and the adjective, however, the base infinitive form (*bi*) is often used after *aggo* (*ooh* or *aggo*) and *gweeh*. For example:

55

Jamaican Creole	English
Yuh <u>aggo bi</u> **very** sick.	You <u>are going to be</u> **very** sick.
Jim <u>gweeh bi</u> **soh** happy.	Jim <u>is going to be</u> **so** happy.
Im <u>aggo</u> **muosli** bi glad fiit.	He <u>is going to</u> **mostly** be glad for it.

The Verb Is Irregular In The Future Tense In The Following Ways:

1. The verb is conjugated *deh* when used directly before prepositions such as *a* (E. *at*), *pau, (E. on) pan* (E. *on*), *inna* (E. *in*), *oova* (E. *over*), *anda* (E. *under*), etc., and adverbs such as *ya* (E. *here*), *deh* (E. *there*), *dyer* (E. *there*), etc., that indicate position or location. For example:

Jamaican Creole	English
Mi <u>aggo deh</u> a karaoke tonight.	I <u>am going to be</u> at karaoke tonight.
Shi <u>a goh deh</u> inna Negril.	She <u>is going to be</u> in Negril.
Wi <u>aggo deh</u> deh.	We <u>are going to be</u> there.

2. It is not uncommon for speakers of Jamaican Creole to totally dispose of the verb before *inna* (E. *in*), *oova* (E. *over*), *anda* (E. *under*), *dong* (E. *down*), *agens* (E. *against*), *afta* (E. *after*), and *aaf* (E. *off*), however. For example:

Jamaican Creole	English
Wi <u>gweeh</u> inna di store.	We <u>will be</u> in the store.
Mi <u>aggo</u> dong deh till yuh come.	I <u>will be</u> down there until you come.
*Im <u>a goh</u> oova dyer.	He <u>will be</u> over there.

* *Im* is almost always used instead of *iih* before *a goh* (*aggo*) and other words beginning with *a*, but E. *him* (used to mean *he* and *him*) is most often used after *a* or words ending with *a*.

Deh is never omitted before the prepositions *a, pan, pau, deh, dyer,* and *ya*. For example:

Jamaican Creole	English
Mi <u>aggo deh</u> a wok tomorrow.	I <u>will be</u> at work tomorrow.
Di key <u>aggo deh</u> pan di tyeb'l.	The key <u>will be</u> on the table.
Im <u>gweeh deh</u> ya.	He <u>will be</u> here.

Suuh And The Future Tense

When *suuh* (E. *soon*) occurs before a conjugated verb in the future tense, the auxiliary verbs *a goh* (*ooh* or *aggo*) and *gweeh* are often omitted. It should be noted that *suuh* is only used before conjugated verbs. Otherwise, E. *soon* is used. For example:

Jamaican Creole	English
Wi <u>suuh lef</u>.	We [will] soon leave.
Shi <u>suuh realize</u> aar mistyek.	She [will] soon realize her mistake.
Iih <u>suuh come</u>.	He [will] soon come.

Note that certain forms of the future tense, such as *will have* and *will have been* are not used in Jamaican Creole.

The Conditional Future Tense

In English, the conditional future tense is used in two instances:

I. Examples of the conditional future in the first instance include *If he comes today, I will get to see him* and *She will understand <u>when</u> she grows up*. In Jamaican Creole, the conditional future tense is formed like the previous examples. *Wi* (E. *will*) is used in this instance of the conditional future tense. So, the examples would read:

Jamaican Creole	English
If im come tudeh, mi <u>wi get fi</u> siim.	If he comes today, I <u>will get to see</u> him.
Shi <u>wi andastan when</u> shi gruo up.	She <u>will understand when</u> she grows up.

In Jamaican Creole, *if* and *when* clauses are not always stated or are not always necessary to establish that a condition is present. It is nonetheless understood that the future occurrence is not definitely certain and is based on some unstated condition or is a matter of opinion. For example:

Jamaican Creole	English
Wi <u>wi gi</u> dem two dyeh fi lef.	We <u>will (possibly/might) give</u> them two days to leave.
Angela <u>wi tek</u> all a di profit an noh gi wi none.	Angela <u>will (possibly/might) take</u> all of the profit and not give us any.

2. An example of the conditional future in the second instance is *If I were to see him, I <u>would</u> tell him*. In Jamaican Creole, *wudda* (E. *would*) is used to indicate this speculation about the future. For example:

Jamaican Creole	English
If im come tudeh, mi <u>wudda</u> get fi siim.	If he comes today, I <u>would</u> get to see him.
Mi <u>wudda</u> goh a di paati <u>if</u> mi did ha company.	I <u>would</u> go to the party <u>if</u> I had company.

In both English and Jamaican Creole, the *if* clause is not necessary to establish that a condition exists. For example:

Jamaican Creole	English
Mi <u>wudda andastan</u>.	I <u>would understand</u>.
Shi <u>wudda bi</u> wau fool.	She <u>would be</u> a fool.
Nobody <u>wudda nuo</u>.	Nobody <u>would know</u>.

The Verb Bi In The Conditional Future Tense

The auxiliary verbs *wi* and *wudda* are used before the base infinitive form of the verb *bi* to form the conditional future tense. For example:

Jamaican Creole	English
Shi <u>wi bi</u> helpful if yuh nice to aar.	She <u>will (possibly/might) be</u> helpful if you are nice to her.
John <u>wudda bi</u> di jaiva.	John <u>would be</u> the driver.
Simone <u>wi bi</u> yuh fren if yuh gi aar tings.	Simone <u>will (possibly/might) be</u> your friend if you give her things.

It is not uncommon for the verb to be omitted and for *wi* or *wudda* to be retained before adjectives, although in some cases *bi* is used. For example:

Jamaican Creole	English
Nancy <u>wudda upset</u> if yuh did mess up aar dress.	Nancy <u>would be upset</u> if you messed up her dress.
Mi <u>wi lonely</u> if yuh lef mi all by miself.	I <u>will (possibly/might) be lonely</u> if you leave me all by myself.
Susan <u>wi glad</u> fi di chance fi duh soh'mn wid aar life.	Susan <u>will (possibly/might) be glad</u> for the chance to do something with her life.

When there is an intervening adverb between the conjugated verb or verb phrase and the adjective, however, the base infinitive form, *bi,* is used after *wi.* For example:

Jamaican Creole	English
Shi <u>wi bi</u> **very** <u>miserable</u> if yuh tek ih fram aar.	She <u>will (possibly/might) be</u> **very** <u>miserable</u> if you take it from her.
Jim <u>wudda bi</u> **soh** <u>happy</u> if yuh tell im.	Jim <u>would be</u> **so** <u>happy</u> if you [were to] tell him.
Im <u>wudda</u> **likely** <u>bi glad</u> fiit.	He <u>would</u> **likely** <u>be glad</u> for it.

The verb is conjugated *deh* when used directly before prepositions such as *a* (E. *at*), *pau* (E. *on*), *pan* (E. *on*), *inna* (E. *in*), *oova* (E. *over*), *anda* (E. *under*), etc., and adverbs such as *ya* (E. *here*), *deh* (E. *there*), *dyer* (E. *there*), etc., that indicate position or location. For example:

Jamaican Creole	English
Shi <u>wudda deh</u> deh if yuh did a come.	She <u>would be</u> there if you were coming.
Mi <u>wudda deh</u> a karaoke tonight.	I <u>would be</u> at karaoke tonight.
Shane <u>wi deh</u> inna di crowd an yuh noh siim.	Shane <u>will (possibly/might) be</u> in the crowd and you [might] not see him.

It is not uncommon for speakers of Jamaican Creole to totally dispose of the verb before prepositions such as *inna* (E. *in*), *oova* (E. *over*), *anda* (E. *under*), *dong* (E. *down*), *agens* (E. *against*), *afta* (E. *after*), and *aaf* (E. *off*), however. For example:

Jamaican Creole	English
Wi <u>wudda</u> inna di store if yuh come.	We <u>would be</u> in the store if you came.
Mi <u>wi</u> dong deh till yuh come.	I <u>will (possibly/might) be</u> down there until you come.
Im <u>wi</u> oova dyer.	He <u>will (possibly/might) be</u> over there.

Build Your Jamaican Creole Vocabulary:

an/auh *conj.* and

chaah *n., v.* chew

fyek *adj., v.* fake

hyersoh *adv., n.* here

juok *n., v.* joke

lakka seh *conj.* as if

puok *n.* pork

wia *contr.* we are

PRACTICE EXERCISE 11

Translate the following sentences to Jamaican Creole.

1. They are going to work on the project tomorrow.
2. I will give you the book if you want it.
3. The dog will be sick if it eats too much food.
4. Tomorrow is going to be sunny.
5. The boy will graduate soon and go off to university.
6. After we leave here, we will go to Port Antonio.
7. It would be a good day tomorrow if we got to go to the show.
8. My mother and I will have a picnic on the grass at the park.
9. The team is going to be in Christiana tomorrow.
10. I would leave the key on the table in the living room.

Translate the following sentences to English.

1. Mi wudda type up di pyepa fi yuh.
2. Dem aggo goh a class tomorrow afta dem lef di shuo.
3. Di tiicha dem wi meet nex week if all goh well.
4. Shi wi deh inna di bank if yuh aggo meet aar.
5. Dem wi reach by tomorrow if dem lef out now.
6. Sports dyeh aggo bi nex mont.
7. Di class wi duh good inna di tes bikaah all a di pikini dem did study.
8. Mi tink mi aggo lef now.
9. Wi wi tek di bus fi goh a Mandeville bikaah ih faas.
10. Datdeh song aggo goh a nomba one.

Lesson Twelve

When A Verb Phrase Contains An Infinitive

When a verb phrase contains an infinitive, the verb behaves as it does in English. An example of a phrase with an infinitive verb is *has to leave now*. The infinitive verb in the example is *to leave*. In Jamaican Creole, the infinitive verb combines *fi* and the base infinitive form of the verb. An example of this is *fi run* (E. *to run)*. Additional examples include:

Jamaican Creole	*English*
Dem <u>a gi fi receive</u>.	They <u>are giving to receive</u>.
Yuh <u>aggo haffi goh</u>.	You <u>will have to go</u>.
Mi <u>a wyet fi si</u> dem.	I <u>am waiting to see</u> them.

Infinitives And The Verb Bi

The verb *bi* is **never** used before an infinitive verb. Jamaicans would state the sentence in such a way so as to avoid this conjugation. For example, the sentence *She is to know the result soon* might be stated *Shi aggo nuo di result soon* (E. *She will know the result soon*).

The verb behaves regularly in all other instances and is used in its infinitive form **after** a conjugated verb or auxiliary verb (except before adjectives and prepositions as discussed below). For example:

Jamaican Creole	*English*
Wi <u>huop fi bi</u> im fren.	We <u>hope to be</u> his friend.
Mi <u>wau yuh fi bi</u> silent.	I <u>want you to be</u> silent.
Shi <u>a expek fi bi</u> di fos one.	She <u>is expecting to be</u> the first one.

Prepositions And The Verb Fi Bi

The verb *fi bi* (E. *to be*) is irregular when used directly before prepositions such as *a* (E. *at*), *pau* (E. *on*), *pan* (E. *on*), *inna* (E. *in*), *oova* (E, *over*), *anda* (E. *under*), etc., and adverbs such as *ya* (E. *here*), *deh* (E. *there*), etc., that indicate position or location and becomes *fi deh* when used before them. In most instances, the sentence is usually indicating the physical location or position of the subject. For example:

Jamaican Creole	*English*
Mi <u>wau fi deh</u> a di paati.	I <u>want to be</u> at the party.
Sheila <u>expek fi deh pan</u> top always.	Sheila <u>expects to be on</u> top always.
Ih <u>look better fi deh inna</u> di box.	It <u>looks better [for it] to be</u> in the box.

Despite this general rule, however, it is not uncommon for speakers of Jamaican Creole to totally dispose of the verb before prepositions such as *inna* (E. *in*), *oova* (E. *over*), *anda* (E. *under*), *dong* (E. *down*), *agens* (E. *against*), *afta* (E. *after*), and *aaf* (E. *off*). *Fi* is retained before the preposition, however. For example:

Jamaican Creole	*English*
Mi <u>wau fi inna</u> di ban.	I <u>want to be</u> in the band.
Sheila <u>expek fi afta</u> him.	Sheila <u>expects to be after</u> him.
Ih <u>look better fi inna</u> di box.	It <u>looks better [for it] to be</u> in the box.

Fi deh is always used before *a, pan, pau, deh, dyer,* and *ya*. For example:

Jamaican Creole	English
Mi <u>wau fi deh a</u> wok.	I <u>want to be at</u> work.
Shi <u>huop fi deh deh</u>.	She <u>hopes to be there</u>.
It <u>ha fi deh pan</u> di shelf.	It <u>has to be on</u> the shelf.

Adjectives And The Verb Fi Bi

The verb *fi bi* can either be used or omitted when it occurs in its infinitive form before an adjective. Note, however, that *fi* (E. *to*) is retained before the adjective even if the verb is omitted. For example:

Jamaican Creole	English
Im <u>seem fi bi strong</u>.	He <u>seems to be strong</u>.
Shi <u>haffi naive</u> fi believe dat.	She <u>has to be naive</u> to believe that.
Mi <u>wish fi happy</u>.	I <u>wish to be happy</u>.

Note that if an adverb modifies the adjective, the above rule still stands. For example:

Jamaican Creole	English
Im <u>seem fi bi **very** strong</u>.	He <u>seems to be **very** strong</u>.
Shi <u>haffi **very** naive</u> fi believe dat.	She <u>has to be **very** naive</u> to believe that.
Mi <u>wish fi **totally** happy</u>.	I <u>wish to be **totally** happy</u>.

When an adjective relates to nationality, the verb is always used in its infinitive form. For example:

Jamaican Creole	English
Margarita <u>a apply fi bi</u> Cuban.	Margarita <u>is applying to be</u> Cuban.
Shi <u>wau fi bi</u> Jamaican.	She <u>wants to be</u> Jamaican.

Infinitive Verbs Used After The Verb Goh

When an infinitive occurs after the verb *goh* (E. *go*) in the continuous present tense, the continuous past tense, the future tense, and the conditional future tense, the infinitive verb becomes irregular. In these cases, the verb is used in its base infinitive form instead of its infinitive form. For example:

The Continuous Present Tense

Jamaican Creole	*English*
Dem <u>a goh iht</u>.	They <u>are going to eat</u>.
Shi <u>a goh goh</u> a school.	She <u>is going to go</u> to school.
Im <u>a goh learn</u> Spanish.	He <u>is going to learn</u> Spanish.

The Continuous Past Tense

Jamaican Creole	*English*
Di pikni dem <u>did a goh wash</u> di kyaar.	The children <u>were going to wash</u> the car.
Mi <u>did a goh goh</u> a gym.	I <u>was going to go</u> to the gym.
Dem <u>did a goh study</u>.	They <u>were going to study</u>.

The Future Tense

Jamaican Creole	*English*
Shi <u>a goh goh</u> a wok.	She <u>is going to go</u> to work.
Wi <u>gweeh goh help</u> dem.	We <u>will go to help</u> them.
Dem <u>a goh si</u> wa mi did a talk bout.	They <u>are going to see</u> what I was talking about.

The Conditional Future Tense

Jamaican Creole	*English*
Shi <u>wudda goh sleep</u>.	She <u>would go to sleep</u>.
Wi <u>wudda goh help</u> dem.	We <u>would go to help</u> them.
Dem <u>wi goh si</u> aar.	They <u>will (possibly/might) go to see</u> her.

Inserting *fi* before the verb that follows *goh* would change the meaning of the sentence. Inserting *fi* after *goh* in the continuous present tense, the continuous past tense, the future tense, and the conditional future tense changes the meaning of *fi* to *in order to*. For example:

Jamaican Creole	*English*
Dem <u>did a goh fi iht</u>.	They <u>were going in order to eat</u>.
Wi <u>wi goh fi help</u> dem.	We <u>will go in order to help</u> them.
Im <u>a goh fi learn</u> Spanish.	He <u>is going in order to learn</u> Spanish.

Infinitive Verbs Used After The Verb Wau

When an infinitive verb follows the verb *wau* (E. *want*), *fi* can either be used or eliminated altogether (although it is most times eliminated). For example:

Jamaican Creole	*English*
John <u>wau nuo</u> weh yuh deh.	John <u>wants to know</u> where you are.
Di pikni dem <u>wau wash</u> di kyaar.	The children <u>want to wash</u> the car.
Yuh <u>ha fi wau fi succeed</u> muo dau eniting.	You <u>have to want to succeed</u> more than anything.

Build Your Jamaican Creole Vocabulary:

aal *adv., prep.* even; regarding

baamyaad *n.* a place where obeah is practiced

choo-cho/chuo-cho *n.* chayote

ih *adj., pron.* it; its; the

jonjo *n.* mold

ku ya *interj.* look here

qwaaril *n., v.* quarrel

wadyeh/wedyeh *n.* the other day

PRACTICE EXERCISE 12

Translate the following sentences to Jamaican Creole.

1. She likes to sing.
2. We eat to be healthy.
3. He is going to go to the barbershop.
4. The children are starting to learn to read.
5. Suzie went to see the doctor after going to pay the bills.
6. The man was hoping to find a friend.
7. She will try to do it.
8. They are hoping to replace the old battery with a new one soon.
9. The car swerved to avoid the post.
10. He has to know the truth so that he can make the right decision.

Translate the following sentences to English.

1. Mi granny like fi cook.
2. Dem wau duh good inna di competition.
3. Wi a study fi pass di exam.
4. Di byebi a goh sleep.
5. Di bwuay dem did wau fi si di principal.
6. Dem did a huop fi hyeh di outcome, but dem did haffi lef.
7. Shi a goh finish di wok soh shi kyah sleep.
8. Dem wudda like fi op'mn wau new store.
9. Iih wau fi finalize evriting bifuo iih lef di country.
10. Wi expek fi siim nex week.

Lesson Thirteen

The Passive Voice

An example of the passive voice in English is *The ball is being kicked by the boy*. Although the boy is kicking the ball, the ball is presented as the subject of the sentence. Other examples include *He has been seen by the doctor* and *The rat got eaten by the cat*. In Jamaican Creole, the verbs *bi* and *ha* are not used before the past participle (as is consistent with the present perfect tense), and *get* is only used in rare cases. For example:

Jamaican Creole	*English*
Di fish skyel by Peter.	The fish was scaled by Peter.
Di toy brok by di byebi.	The toy was broken by the baby.
Iih get beat up by iih schoolmate.	He got beaten up by his schoolmate.

Sometimes the doer of the action is obscured. For example:

Jamaican Creole	*English*
Di fish skyel.	The fish was scaled.
Di toy brok.	The toy was broken.
Iih get beat up.	He got beaten up.

The Impersonal Passive Voice

In the impersonal passive voice of English, one would say *It is expected that he will recover* instead of *We expect that he will recover.* Jamaican Creole also uses the impersonal passive voice by employing *a* (E. *it is*) or *a did/a beeh/ a weeh/ a beeh did/a weeh did* (E. *it was*) at the beginning of the sentence. This is done for two reasons. The first reason is to emphasize some aspect of the sentence, such as the subject, object acted upon, the action done, or an adjective describing the subject (sometimes due to impatience or irritation). The second reason is in response to questions. Deciding which verb or phrase to stress depends on what needs to be emphasized. The conjunction *dat* and the pronoun *who* are usually omitted in these sentences and are therefore understood.

If one wants the attention to be drawn to the subject of a sentence, *a* or *a did* (and to a lesser extent *a beeh, a weeh, a beeh did,* or *a weeh did*) is placed before the subject noun or pronoun that is being emphasized. *A did* (*a beeh, a weeh, a beeh did,* or *a weeh did*) indicates that the event or action took place in the past, even if other verbs in the predicate are used in the present tense. Verbs used in the past tense in the predicate would make the entire sentence past, even if *a* is used at the beginning of the sentence. Let us say someone did something bad, and you were being blamed for it. You want it to be known that it was John who did the bad thing. Instead of simply saying *John did dwiit,* most people would say *A John did dwiit* (E. *It was John [who] did it*). The emphasis is thus placed on John. Words in parentheses in the English translation are inserted to give clearer meaning to the sentence. For example:

Jamaican Creole	English
A did di cat iht di fish dis maanin.	It was the cat [that] ate the fish this morning.
A him a goh goh a wok.	It is he [who] is going to go to work.
A beeh him pyeh mi five dalla fiit.	It was he [who] paid me five dollars for it.

If one wants the attention to be drawn to a noun or pronoun that is not the subject of the sentence, then the sentence is reconstructed and *a* or *a did* (and to a lesser extent *a beeh, a weeh, a beeh did*, or *a weeh did*) is placed before the noun or pronoun being emphasized at the beginning of the sentence. For example:

Jamaican Creole	English
A did dis maanin di cat iht di fish.	It was this morning [that] the cat ate the fish.
A wok him a goh goh.	It is work [that] he is going to go [to].
A mi him pyeh five dalla fiit.	It is I [whom] he paid five dollars for it.

If one wants to emphasize the subject's action, then the sentence is reconstructed so that the verb that describes the action being emphasized is stated first. This format is not used in English. The sentence can be constructed in two ways:

1. *A* or *a did* (and to a lesser extent *a beeh, a weeh, a beeh did*, or *a weeh did*) is placed before the verb describing the action being emphasized and is used at the beginning of the sentence. This verb will also be repeated in the predicate of the sentence, although the tense might change to indicate when the action takes place. If it is part of a verb phrase in the predicate, it is usually the first verb mentioned. As indicated previously, *a did* indicates that the

event or action took place in the past, even if other verbs in the predicate are used in the present tense. For example:

Jamaican Creole	English
A help im did a try fi help.	lit. It is help [that] he was trying to help. (*He was trying to help*).
A goh im did a goh.	lit. It is go [that] he was going. (*He was going*).
A weeh did run im a run an jump when im fall pan im fyes.	lit. It was run [that] he was running and jumping when he fall on his face. (*He was running and jumping when he fell on his face*).

2. The verb that describes the action being emphasized is mentioned before being included in the sentence. In this case *a* or *a did* (*a beeh, a weeh, a beeh did*, or *a weeh did*) is **not** placed before the verb. The verb is used in its base infinitive form regardless of the tense it will acquire in the sentence. It would appear that this version is merely an abbreviation of the previous construction. For example:

Jamaican Creole	English
Kick im did a kick di ball.	lit. Kick [that] he was kicking the ball. (*He was kicking the ball*).
Run iih did run.	lit. Run [that] he had run. (*He had run*).
Plyeh im a plyeh.	lit. Play [that] he is playing. (*He is playing*).

If one wants to emphasize an adjective describing the subject, then one of two things can be done:

1. *A* or *a did* (and to a lesser extent *a beeh, a weeh, a beeh did*, or *a weeh did*) is placed before the adjective that describes the subject at the beginning of the sentence. This is one of the rare instances where the verb *bi* is used before an adjective. This adjective will also be repeated in the predicate of the sentence. Notice though, that the verb *bi* is absent in the predicate. If more than one adjective describe the subject, the first mentioned is usually the one emphasized. For example:

Jamaican Creole	English
<u>A tontid</u> im tontid.	lit. <u>It is dizzy</u> [that] he is dizzy. (*He is dizzy*).
<u>A beeh did happy</u> Melissa happy.	<u>It was happy</u> [that] Melissa was happy. (*Melissa was happy*).
<u>A hungry</u> iih did hungry auh taiyad.	<u>It is hungry</u> [that] he was hungry and tired. (*He was hungry and tired*).

2. The adjective can also be used at the beginning of the sentence, and it is repeated in the predicate (except that *a* or *a did* (*a beeh, a weeh, a beeh did*, or *a weeh did*) is not used at the beginning of the sentence). This formation is an abbreviation of the first construction. For example:

Jamaican Creole	English
<u>Funny</u> deeh funny.	lit. <u>Funny</u> they are funny. (*They are funny*).
<u>Upset</u> im did upset.	lit. <u>Upset</u> he was upset. (*He was upset*).
<u>Big</u> aar bag big auh heavy.	lit. <u>Big</u> her bag is big and heavy. (*Her bag is big and heavy*).

Build Your Jamaican Creole Vocabulary:

aam *n., v.* armpit

badbrok *v.* spoilt

egzop *adj.* meddlesome

faama *n.* farmer

galang *interj., v.* go on; behave (in a particular manner)

kyaah *mod. aux., v.* cannot; carry

wamek *adj.* why

PRACTICE EXERCISE 13

Rewrite the following sentences to the passive voice in Jamaican Creole. For each sentence, attempt to emphasize the subject of the sentence, a noun or a pronoun in the predicate of the sentence, and a verb describing an action performed by the subject.

1. The dog bit the cat.
2. It costs ten dollars to buy the mangoes.
3. Shawn did it.
4. Peter is fixing the car.
5. We take the bus to school every day.
6. Her aunt came yesterday.
7. It is not good.
8. The baby is crying.
9. He is the number one batsman.
10. Faith broke the window above her bed.

Translate the following sentences to English.

1. A di blue kyaar shi love.
2. A pick dem did a pick guava.
3. Dotti di sheet dotti.
4. Oh'mn di duo did oh'mn when mi try ih.
5. Gi im did gi wi di daag.
6. A weeh did fain dem fain ih.
7. A ong'l one apple deh pan di tree.
8. Fret im a fret.
9. A Jody kyaah dance!
10. Di pyepa wet by di laas sumaddi weh did deh inna di room.

Lesson Fourteen

Making A Sentence Negative

Examples of negative sentences in English include: *He is not here*; *We do not know*; *I will not see him*; and *You should not do that.*
The negative auxiliary verbs used in Jamaican Creole include *noh, dooh, duo, neva* (sometimes used as *nebba* or *neeh*), *neva did* (sometimes used as *nebba did* or *neeh did*), *naah*, E. *not iiv'n* (sometimes used as *niiv'n, neev'n,* or *noh iiv'n*), E. *not iiv'n did* (sometimes used as *niiv'n did, neev'n did,* or *noh iiv'n did*), *wud'na*, and *cud'na* (sometimes used as *cud'n did* or *cud'na did*). The negative auxiliary verb used depends on the tense of the verb it modifies. In Jamaican Creole, the negative modal auxiliaries are *wud'n, naah goh, wi noh* (or *noh wi*), *shud'n, kyaah, cud'n*, E. *might noh, noh fi* (or *noffi*), and *mos'n*.

Negative Auxiliary Verbs

Noh, Dooh, And Duo

Noh, dooh, and *duo* are associated with the present tense. *Noh* means *not, does not, do not, has not,* and *have not* and is used with the base infinitive form of the verb. *Dooh* and *duo* mean *does not, do not, has not,* and *have not*, and they are also used with the base infinitive form of the verb. They are, however, used to a lesser extent than is *noh*. For example:

Jamaican Creole	English
Mi <u>noh dwiit</u> yet.	I <u>have not done</u> it yet.
Deeh <u>noh ha</u> wa ih tek.	They <u>do not have</u> what it takes.
Iih <u>dooh siit</u>.	He <u>does not see</u> it.

The Verb Bi Is Irregular When Used With Noh

The verb *bi* is conjugated *a* when used with *noh*. Together, *a* and *noh* mean *am not, is not,* and *are not*. For example:

Jamaican Creole	English
Shi <u>a noh</u> di president.	She <u>is not</u> the president.
Dem <u>a noh</u> paat a di group.	They <u>are not</u> part of the group.
Im <u>a noh</u> di one weh yuh wau.	He <u>is not</u> the one that you want.

When the verb would have occurred with *noh* before an adjective, the verb is omitted and only *noh* is used. For example:

Jamaican Creole	English
Dem <u>noh</u> good.	They <u>are not</u> good.
Mi <u>noh</u> well.	I <u>am not</u> well.
Di house <u>noh</u> blue.	The house <u>is not</u> blue.

When used before prepositions such as *a* (E. *at*), *pau* (E. *on*), *pan* (E. *on*), *inna* (E. *in*), *oova* (E, *over*), *anda* (E. *under*), etc., and adverbs such as *ya* (E. *here*), *deh* (E. *there*), *dyer* (E. *there*), etc., the verb becomes *deh*. For example:

Jamaican Creole	English
Shi <u>noh deh</u> ya.	She <u>is not</u> here.
Dem <u>noh deh</u> inna di building.	They <u>are not</u> in the building.
Mi <u>noh deh</u> inna di store.	I <u>am not</u> in the store.

It is not uncommon for speakers of Jamaican Creole to totally dispose of the verb before *inna, oova, anda,* and *dong.* An example of this is *Mi noh inna di store* (E. *I am not in the store*).

Naah

Naah is used to indicate what is not currently taking place. In English, this is the present continuous tense. It means *is not* or *are not.* For example:

Jamaican Creole	English
Nancy <u>naah sleep</u> yet.	Nancy <u>is not sleeping</u> yet.
Wi <u>naah pyeh</u> dem di money.	We <u>are not paying</u> them the money.
Trisha <u>naah goh</u> a di mall wid aar madda.	Trisha <u>is not going</u> to the mall with her mother.

The Verb Bi And Naah

The verb *bi* is used in its base infinitve form when associated with *naah.* For example:

Jamaican Creole	English
Unnu <u>naah bi</u> fyer.	You <u>are not being</u> fair.
John <u>naah bi</u> haness.	John <u>is not being</u> honest.

Not liv'n (Niiv'n, Neev'n, Or Noh liv'n)

Not iiv'n (sometimes used as *niiv'n, neev'n,* or *noh iiv'n*) is associated with the present tense, the present perfect tense, and the past tense. *Not iiv'n* (*niiv'n, neev'n,* or *noh iiv'n*) means *does not even, do not even, has not even, have not even,* and *did not even. Noh iiv'n* is **not** frequently used to mean *did not even.* For example:

Jamaican Creole	English
Wi <u>not iiv'n showa</u> yet.	We <u>have not even showered</u> yet.
Iih <u>niiv'n nuo</u>.	He <u>does not even know</u>.
Dem <u>neev'n seh sorry</u>.	They <u>did not even say sorry</u>.

The Verb Bi When Used With Not Iiv'n, Niiv'n, Neev'n, Or Noh Iiv'n

When the verb *bi* is used with *not iiv'n, niiv'n, neev'n,* or *noh iiv'n*, it is conjugated *a*. Together, *a* and *not iiv'n (niiv'n, neev'n,* or *noh iiv'n)* mean *am not even, is not even,* and *are not even*. Note that the verb *a* can come before or after *not iiv'n, niiv'n, neev'n,* and *noh iiv'n*. For example:

Jamaican Creole	English
Shi <u>not iiv'n a</u> ten.	lit. She <u>not even is</u> ten. (*She is not even ten*).
Mi <u>a neev'n</u> aar fren.	I <u>am not even</u> her friend.
<u>A niiv'n</u> ten a'clak.	It <u>is not even</u> ten o'clock.

When used before prepositions such as *a* (E. *at*), *pau* (E. *on*), *pan* (E. *on*), *inna* (E. *in*), *oova* (E. *over*), *anda* (E. *under*), etc., and adverbs such as *ya* (E. *here*), *deh* (E. *there*), *dyer* (E. *there*), etc., that indicate the location or position of the subject, the verb is conjugated *deh*. For example:

Jamaican Creole	English
Deeh <u>noh iiv'n deh</u> ya.	They <u>are not even</u> here.
Mi bredda <u>niiv'n deh</u> huom.	My brother <u>is not even</u> home.
Shi <u>neev'n deh</u> inna di affis.	She <u>is not even</u> in the office.

It is not uncommon for speakers of Jamaican Creole to totally dispose of the verb before *inna, oova, anda,* and *dong*. An example is *Tom niiv'n oova dyer* (E. *Tom is not even over there*).

When the verb would have occurred with *not iiv'n, niiv'n, neev'n,* or *noh iiv'n* before an adjective, the verb is omitted and only *not iiv'n, niiv'n, neev'n,* or *noh iiv'n* is used. For example:

Jamaican Creole	English
Im <u>not iiv'n</u> funny.	He <u>is not even</u> funny.
Deeh <u>neev'n</u> sick.	They <u>are not even</u> sick.
Shi <u>niiv'n</u> happy.	She <u>is not even</u> happy.

Not Iiv'n Did (Niiv'n Did, Neev'n Did, Or Noh Iiv'n Did)

Not iiv'n did (sometimes used as *niiv'n did, neev'n did,* or *noh iiv'n did*) is associated with the past tense and past perfect tense. It means *did not even* and *had not even.* For example:

Jamaican Creole	English
Iih <u>not iiv'n did siit</u>.	He <u>had not even seen</u> it.
Shi <u>neev'n did wok</u> laas week.	She <u>did not even work</u> last week.
Im <u>noh iiv'n did duh</u> it.	He <u>had not even done</u> it.

The Verb Bi When Used With Not Iiv'n Did, Niiv'n Did, Neev'n Did, Or Noh Iiv'n Did

When the verb *bi* is used with *not iiv'n did, niiv'n did, neev'n did,* or *noh iiv'n did,* it is conjugated *a.* Together, *a* and *not iiv'n did* (*niiv'n did, neev'n did,* or *noh iiv'n did*) mean *was not even, were not even,* and *had not even been.* Note that *a* comes after *not iiv'n did, niiv'n did, neev'n did,* and *noh iiv'n did* in the sentence except when the subject of the verb is *ih* (E. *it*). In this case, *a* comes before *not iiv'n did, niiv'n did, neev'n did,* and *noh iiv'n did.* For example:

Jamaican Creole	English
Mi <u>neev'n did a</u> aar fren.	I <u>was not even</u> her friend.
Dem <u>not iiv'n did a</u> di bes back den.	They <u>had not even been</u> the best back then.
<u>A noh iiv'n did</u> da one deh.	It <u>was not even</u> that one.

When used before prepositions such as *a* (E. *at*), *pau* (E. *on*), *pan* (E. *on*), *inna* (E. *in*), *oova* (E. *over*), *anda* (E. *under*), etc., and adverbs such as *ya* (E. *here*), *deh* (E. *there*), *dyer* (E. *there*), etc., that indicate the location or position of the subject, the verb becomes *deh*. For example:

Jamaican Creole	English
Deeh <u>niiv'n did deh</u> ya.	They <u>had not even been</u> here.
Mi bredda <u>neev'n did deh</u> huom.	My brother <u>had not even been</u> home.
Shi <u>noh iiv'n did deh</u> inna di affis.	She <u>had not even been</u> in the office.

It is not uncommon for speakers of Jamaican Creole to totally dispose of the verb before *inna, oova, anda*, and *dong*. An example is *Di envelope not iiv'n did inna di bag* (E. *The envelope had not even been in the bag*).

When the verb *bi* is indicating the state of the subject (as indicated by an adjective), the verb is omitted and only *not iiv'n did, niiv'n did, neev'n did,* or *noh iiv'n did* is used. For example:

Jamaican Creole	English
Im <u>niiv'n did</u> frai'n.	He <u>was not even</u> frightened.
Deeh <u>neev'n did</u> ripe.	They <u>had not even been</u> ripe.
Di car <u>not iiv'n did</u> yellow.	The car <u>was not even</u> yellow.

Neva (Nebba Or Neeh)

Neva (sometimes used as *nebba* or *neeh*) is associated with the present perfect tense and past tense. It means *did not, has never,* and *have never*. For example:

82

Jamaican Creole	English
Iih <u>neeh iht</u>.	He <u>did not eat</u>.
Dem <u>neva wok</u> a night, eva.	They <u>have never worked</u> at night, ever.
Im <u>nebba duh</u> noh'n good inna im life.	He <u>has never done</u> anything good in his life.

The Verb Bi When Used With Neva (Nebba Or Neeh)

When the verb *bi* is used with *neva*, *nebba*, and *neeh*, it is conjugated *a*. Together, *a* and *neva* (*nebba* or *neeh*) mean *is never, are never, was not, were not, was never,* and *were never*. Note that the verb *a* can be placed before or after *neva*, *nebba*, and *neeh*. When used with *ih* or E. *it*, *a* is always placed before *neva*, *nebba*, and *neeh*. For example:

Jamaican Creole	English
Wi <u>a neva</u> di fos.	We <u>were not</u> the first.
Shi <u>neva a</u> di bes.	She <u>never was</u> the best.
<u>A neeh</u> da one deh.	It <u>was not</u> that one.

When used before prepositions such as *a* (E. *at*), *pau* (E. *on*), *pan* (E. *on*), *inna* (E. *in*), *oova* (E. *over*), *anda* (E. *under*), etc., and adverbs such as *ya* (E. *here*), *deh* (E. *there*), *dyer* (E. *there*), etc., that indicate the location or position of the subject, the verb is conjugated *deh*. For example:

Jamaican Creole	English
Deeh <u>neva deh</u> ya, eva.	They <u>are never</u> here, ever.
Mi bredda <u>nebba deh</u> huom.	My brother <u>is never</u> home.
Shi <u>neeh deh</u> inna di affis.	She <u>was not</u> in the office.

It is not uncommon for speakers of Jamaican Creole to totally dispose of the verb before *inna*, *oova*, *anda*, and *dong*. An example is *Tom neva oova dyer* (E. *Tom was not over there*).

When the verb would have occurred with *neva* (*neeh* or *nebba*) before an adjective, the verb is omitted and only *neva*, *nebba*, or *neeh* is used. For example:

Jamaican Creole	English
Im <u>neeh</u> funny.	He <u>was not</u> funny.
Deeh <u>neva</u> clean.	They <u>are never</u> clean.
Shi <u>nebba</u> untidy.	She <u>was never</u> untidy.

Neva Did (Nebba Did Or Neeh Did)

Neva did (sometimes used as *nebba did* or *neeh did*) is associated with the past tense and past perfect tense. It means *did not*, *had not*, and *had never*. For example:

Jamaican Creole	English
Iih <u>neva did siit</u> before in im life.	He <u>had never seen</u> it before in his life.
Shi <u>neeh did wok</u> laas week.	She <u>did not work</u> last week.
Im <u>nebba did duh</u> it.	He <u>had not done</u> it.

The Verb Bi When Used With Neva Did (Nebba Did Or Neeh Did)

When the verb *bi* is used with *neva did*, *nebba did*, or *neeh did*, it is conjugated *a*. Together, *neva did* (*nebba did* or *neeh did*) and *a* mean *was not*, *were not*, *was never*, *were never*, *had not been*, and *had never been*. Note that *a* comes after *neva did*, *nebba did*, and *neeh did* in the sentence except when the verb would have been preceded by *ih* (E. *it*). For example:

Jamaican Creole	English
Mi <u>neva did a</u> aar fren.	I <u>was never</u> her friend.
Dem <u>neva did a</u> di bes back den.	They <u>had not been</u> the best back then.
A <u>neeh did</u> da one deh.	It <u>was not</u> that one.

When used before prepositions such as *a* (E. *at*), *pau* (E. *on*), *pan* (E. *on*), *inna* (E. *in*), *oova* (E. *over*), *anda* (E. *under*), etc., and adverbs such as *ya* (E. *here*), *deh* (E. *there*), *dyer* (E. *there*), etc., that indicate the location or position of the subject, the verb becomes *deh*. For example:

Jamaican Creole	English
Deeh <u>neva did deh</u> huom.	They <u>had not been</u> home.
Mi bredda <u>neeh did deh</u> a di gyem.	My brother <u>had not been</u> at the game.
Pam <u>neeh did deh</u> inna di building.	Pam <u>had not been</u> in the building.

It is not uncommon for speakers of Jamaican Creole to totally dispose of the verb before *inna, oova, anda,* and *dong*. An example is *Di envelope neva did inna di bag* (E. *The envelope had not been in the bag*).

When the verb *bi* is indicating the state of the subject (as indicated by an adjective), the verb is omitted and only *neva did, nebba did,* or *neeh did* is used. For example:

Jamaican Creole	English
Im <u>neva did</u> frai'n.	He <u>was not</u> frightened.
Deeh <u>neva did</u> frenli.	They <u>had not been</u> friendly.
Shi <u>neeh did</u> busy.	She <u>was not</u> busy.

Wud'na

Wud'na is associated with the present perfect tense (review if necessary). It means *would not have*. It is used in Jamaican Creole as it is in English. For example:

Jamaican Creole	English
Mi <u>wud'na</u> siit if yuh neva did tell mi.	I <u>would not have</u> seen it if you had not told me.
John <u>wud'na</u> gi yuh.	John <u>would not have</u> given [it to] you.
Di people dem <u>wud'na</u> enta di building.	The people <u>would not have</u> entered the building.

Wud'na And The Verb Bi

Wud'na is used with the verb *bi* to mean *would not have been*. The verb *bi* is generally used in its base infinitive form. The verb becomes *deh* when used directly before prepositions such as *a* (E. *at*), *pau* (E. *on*), *pan* (E. *on*), *inna* (E. *in*), *oova* (E. *over*), *anda* (E. *under*), etc., and adverbs such as *ya* (E. *here*), *deh* (E. *there*), *dyer* (E. *there*), etc., that indicate position or location. The verb is sometimes disposed of before adjectives, and *wud'na* is abbreviated *wud'n* before them whether or not the verb is omitted.

The verb is sometimes disposed of before *inna* (E. *in*), *oova* (E. *over*), *anda* (E. *under*), *dong* (E. *down*), *agens* (E. *against*), *afta* (E. *after*), and *aaf* (E. *off*). *Wud'na* is also abbreviated *wud'n* before these prepositions whether or not the verb is omitted. The verb is **never** omitted before *a*, *pan*, *pau*, *deh*, *dyer*, and *ya*. For example:

Jamaican Creole	English
Dem <u>wud'n</u> happy wid dat if yuh did tell dem.	They <u>would not have been</u> happy with that if you had told them.
Pam <u>wud'na bi</u> aar fren if shi neva rich.	Pam <u>would not have been</u> her friend if she wasn't rich.
Di people dem <u>wud'na deh</u> deh.	The people <u>would not have been</u> there.

Cud'na

Cud'na (sometimes used as *cud'n did* or *cud'na did*) is associated with the present perfect tense (review if necessary). It means *could not have*. It is used in Jamaican Creole as it is in English. For example:

Jamaican Creole	*English*
Pete <u>cud'na</u> expek wi fi nuo.	Pete <u>could not have</u> expected us to know.
Im <u>cud'na did</u> si roun di ben.	He <u>could not have</u> seen around the bend/corner.
Wi <u>cud'na</u> lef early.	We <u>could not have</u> left early.

Cud'na And The Verb Bi

Cud'na (sometimes used as *cud'n did* or *cud'na did*) is used with the verb *bi* to mean *could not have been*. The verb *bi* is generally used in its base infinitive form. The verb becomes *deh* when used directly before prepositions such as *a* (E. *at*), *pau* (E. *on*), *pan* (E. *on*), *inna* (E. *in*), *oova* (E. *over*), *anda* (E. *under*), etc., and adverbs such as *ya* (E. *here*), *deh* (E. *there*), *dyer* (E. *there*), etc., that indicate position or location.

The verb is sometimes disposed of before adjectives. The verb is sometimes disposed of before *inna* (E. *in*), *oova* (E. *over*), *anda* (E. *under*), *dong* (E. *down*), *agens* (E. *against*), *afta* (E. *after*), and *aaf* (E. *off*). The verb is **never** omitted before *a, pan, pau, deh, dyer*, and *ya*. For example:

Jamaican Creole	*English*
Alan <u>cud'n did</u> happy wid dat.	Alan <u>could not have been</u> happy with that.
Ih <u>cud'na bi</u> di fos time dem a meet.	It <u>could not have been</u> the first time [that] they are meeting.
Mi <u>cud'n deh</u> a church laas night.	I <u>could not have been</u> at church last night.

The Negative Passive Voice

The negative passive voice in Jamaican Creole is formed by using *a noh*, *a neva* (also used as *a nebba* or *a neeh*), *a noh did*, and *a neva did* (also used as *a nebba did* or *a neeh did*) at the beginning of the sentence.

A noh means *it is not*. For example:

Jamaican Creole	English
A <u>noh</u> true wa dem seh.	<u>It is not</u> true what they say.
A <u>noh</u> soh ih goh.	lit. <u>It is not</u> how it goes. (*That's not how it is*).
A <u>noh</u> him dem wau.	<u>It is not</u> he [who] they want.

A neva (*a nebba* or *a neeh*), *a noh did*, and *a neva did* (*a nebba did* or *a neeh did*) mean *it was not*. For example:

Jamaican Creole	English
A <u>neva</u> true wa dem seh.	<u>It was not</u> true what they said.
A <u>noh did</u> soh ih goh.	lit. <u>It was not</u> how it went. (*That was not how it was*).
A <u>neva did</u> him dem wau.	<u>It was not</u> he [who] they wanted.

The Negative Modal Auxiliary Verbs

Some modal auxiliaries require *noh* to form their negative. These include *wi*, E. *might*, and *fi*.

Wi Noh

You will recall from *Lesson Eleven* that *wi* (E. *will*) is used in the conditional future tense along with the *if* or *when* clause. You will also remember that in Jamaican Creole the *if* or *when* clause is not always stated or is not always necessary to establish that a condition is present (review if necessary). *Wi noh* (sometimes used as *noh wi*) means *will not* and is the negative version of *wi*. For example:

Jamaican Creole	*English*
Mi <u>wi noh</u> badda goh.	I <u>will (possibly/might) not</u> bother to go.
Pete <u>wi noh</u> siit lakka how yuh siit.	Pete <u>will (possibly/might) not</u> see it like how you see it.
Iiv'n if Sherry ha wau tes tomorrow, shi <u>noh wi</u> badda fi study.	Even if Sherry has a test tomorrow, she <u>will (possibly/ might) not</u> bother to study.

Wi Noh And The Verb Bi

The verb *bi* behaves exactly as it does with the modal auxiliary *wi*. It is used in its base infinitive form, *bi* (e.g., *Wi noh wi bi yuh fren if yuh rude* (E. *We will [possibly] not be your friend if you are rude*)) and is sometimes omitted before adjectives (e.g., *Wi wi bi aarait/Wii aarait* (E. *We will [most likely] be alright*)).

The verb becomes *deh* when used directly before prepositions such as *a* (E. *at*), *pau* (E. *on*), *pan* (E. *on*), *inna* (E. *in*), *oova* (E. *over*), *anda* (E. *under*), etc., and adverbs such as *ya* (E. *here*), *deh* (E. *there*), *dyer* (E. *there*), etc., that indicate position or location (e.g., *Shi wi noh deh deh when yuh goh deh* (E. *She will [possibly] not be there when you go there*)). The verb is sometimes disposed of before *inna* (E. *in*), *oova* (E. *over*), *anda* (E. *under*), *dong* (E. *down*), *agens* (E. *against*), *afta* (E. *after*), and *aaf* (E. *off*). The verb is **never** omitted before *a, pan, pau, dyer,* and *ya*.

Might Noh

Might noh is used in Jamaican Creole as *might not* is used in English. For example:

Jamaican Creole	English
Shi <u>might noh</u> realize wa shi a duh.	She <u>might not</u> realize what she is doing.
Ih <u>might noh</u> bi di syem if dem noh deh deh.	It <u>might not</u> be the same if they are not there.
Jack a lef, but iih fren dem <u>might noh</u> nuo.	Jack is leaving, but his friends <u>might not</u> know.

Might Noh And The Verb Bi

The verb *bi* is used in its base infinitive form after *might noh* (e.g., *might noh bi*) and is usually omitted before adjectives (e.g., Shi *might noh happy wid yuh decision* (E. *She might not be happy with your decision*)). The verb becomes *deh* when used directly before prepositions such as *a* (E. *at*), *pau* (E. *on*), *pan* (E. *on*), *inna* (E. *in*), *oova* (E. *over*), *anda* (E. *under*), etc., and adverbs such as *ya* (E. *here*), *deh* (E. *there*), *dyer* (E. *there*), etc., that indicate position or location (e.g., *might noh deh*). The verb is sometimes disposed of before *inna* (E. *in*), *oova* (E. *over*), *anda* (E. *under*), *dong* (E. *down*), *agens* (E. *against*), *afta* (E. *after*), and *aaf* (E. *off*). The verb is **never** omitted before *a, pan, pau, deh, dyer,* and *ya*.

Noh Fi

Noh fi (*noffi*) means *ought not to* or *should not*. The following are examples of its use:

Jamaican Creole	English
Yuh <u>noffi</u> believe evriting yuh hyeh.	You <u>ought not to</u> believe everything you hear.
Di govament <u>noffi</u> tax di people dem soh much.	The government <u>should not</u> tax the people so much.
Yuh <u>noffi</u> expek im fi chyeng.	You <u>ought not to</u> expect him to change.

Noh Fi And The Verb Bi

The verb *bi* is used in its base infinitive form after *noh fi* (e.g., *noh fi bi*) and is sometimes omitted before adjectives (e.g., *noh fi happy*).

The verb becomes *deh* when used directly before prepositions such as *a* (E. *at*), *pau* (E. *on*), *pan* (E. *on*), *inna* (E. *in*), *oova* (E. *over*), *anda* (E. *under*), etc., and adverbs such as *ya* (E. *here*), *deh* (E. *there*), *dyer* (E. *there*), etc., that indicate position or location (e.g., *noh fi deh*). The verb is sometimes disposed of before *inna* (E. *in*), *oova* (E. *over*), *anda* (E. *under*), *dong* (E. *down*), *agens* (E. *against*), *afta* (E. *after*), and *aaf* (E. *off*). The verb is **never** omitted before *a*, *pan*, *pau*, *deh*, *dyer*, and *ya*.

Naah Goh

Naah goh (sometimes abbreviated *naah*) means *is not going to*, *are not going to*, and *will not*. For example:

Jamaican Creole	*English*
Jamie <u>naah goh rimemba</u> fi feed di cat.	Jamie <u>will not remember</u> to feed the cat.
Mi <u>naah siim</u>.	I <u>will not see</u> him.
Di girl dem <u>naah goh goh</u> pan di school trip.	The girls <u>are not going to go</u> on the school trip.

Naah Goh And The Verb Bi

The verb *bi* is used in its base infinitive form after *naah goh* (e.g., *naah goh bi*) and is sometimes omitted before adjectives (e.g., *naah goh upset*). The verb becomes *deh* when used directly before prepositions such as *a* (E. *at*), *pau* (E. *on*), *pan* (E. *on*), *inna* (E. *in*), *oova* (E. *over*), *anda* (E. *under*), etc., and adverbs such as *ya* (E. *here*), *deh* (E. *there*), *dyer* (E. *there*), etc., that indicate position or location (e.g., *naah goh deh*). The verb is sometimes disposed of before *inna* (E. *in*), *oova* (E. *over*), *anda* (E. *under*), *dong* (E. *down*), *agens* (E. *against*), *afta* (E. *after*), and *aaf* (E. *off*). The verb is **never** omitted before *a*, *pan*, *pau*, *deh*, *dyer*, and *ya*.

The Remaining Modal Auxiliary Verbs

The modal auxiliaries *wud'n* (E. *would not*), *shud'n* (E. *should not*), *cud'n* (E. *could not*), *mos'n* (E. *must not*), and *kyaah* (E. *cannot*) are used as they are in English. For example:

Jamaican Creole	English
Shi <u>wud'n sign</u> di pyepa dem.	She <u>would not sign</u> the papers.
Mi <u>shud'n goh deh</u>.	I <u>should not go</u> there.
James <u>cud'n tell</u> im.	James <u>could not tell</u> him.

The Verb Bi And The Modal Auxiliaries

The verb *bi* is used in its base infinitive form after *wud'n, shud'n, cud'n, mos'n,* and *kyaah* (e.g., *wud'n bi*) and is sometimes omitted before adjectives (e.g., *mos'n sad*). The verb becomes *deh* when used directly before prepositions such as *a* (E. *at*), *pau* (E. *on*), *pan* (E. *on*), *inna* (E. *in*), *oova* (E. *over*), *anda* (E. *under*), etc., and adverbs such as *ya* (E. *here*), *deh* (E. *there*), *dyer* (E. *there*), etc., that indicate position or location (e.g., *cud'n deh*). The verb is sometimes disposed of before *inna* (E. *in*), *oova* (E. *over*), *anda* (E. *under*), *dong* (E. *down*), *agens* (E. *against*), *afta* (E. *after*), and *aaf* (E. *off*). The verb is **never** omitted before *a, pan, pau, deh, dyer,* and *ya*.

The Double Negative Structure Of Jamaican Creole

The double negative structure that is grammatically incorrect in English is the acceptable form in Jamaican Creole. For example, the sentence *I don't know nothing* would be considered ungrammatical in English. This is, however, the structure that is most used in Jamaican Creole. It is thus common to replace positive adjectives, adverbs, and pronouns with negative ones to make a sentence negative. Some of the common ones are listed below.

Table 6: Negative Words Used To Replace Common Adjectives, Adverbs, And Pronouns

	Adjective	Adverb	Pronoun
any (adj., adv., pron.) Replaced in JC. by:	E. no	E. no	E. none
anybody (pron.) Replaced in JC. by:	n/a	n/a	E. nobody
anymore (adv.) Replaced in JC. by:	n/a	noomuo/ nomo	n/a
anything (adv., pron.) Replaced in JC. by:	n/a	noh'n/ noting	noh'n/ noting
anywhere (adv., pron.) Replaced in JC. by:	n/a	nooweh/ noweh	nooweh/ noweh
somebody (pron.) Replaced in JC. by:	n/a	n/a	E. nobody
something (adv., pron.) Replaced in JC. by:	n/a	noh'n/ noting	noh'n/ noting
somewhere (adv., pron.) Replaced in JC. by:	n/a	nooweh/ noweh	n/a

In English, the sentence can be structured so that the verb takes the negative and not the object (e.g., *He does not see anything*). In Jamaican Creole, both the verb and the object take a negative form. For example:

Jamaican Creole	English
Im <u>noh si noting</u>.	lit. He <u>does not see nothing</u>. (*He does not see anything*).
Mi <u>noh wau none</u>.	lit. I <u>don't want none</u>. (*I don't want any*).
Wi <u>naah goh nooweh</u>.	lit. We <u>are not going nowhere</u>. (*We are not going anywhere*).

Likewise, the sentence can be structured so that the object takes the negative in English (e.g., *I have no money*). Both the verb and the object take a negative in Jamaican Creole. For example:

Jamaican Creole	English
Mi <u>noh ha no money</u>.	lit. I <u>don't have no money</u>. (*I have no money*).
<u>No shuga noh deh</u> ya.	lit. <u>No sugar is not</u> here. (*No sugar is here*).
<u>Nobody neva did a expek</u> ih.	lit. <u>Nobody had not been expecting</u> it. (*Nobody had been expecting it*).

Note, a sentence is never started with *dyer* or *deh* (E. *there*). For example, you will never hear a Jamaican say: *Dyer a nobody ya* (E. *There is nobody here*). Instead, the sentence would be constructed: *Nobody noh deh ya* (E. *Nobody is here*).

Build Your Jamaican Creole Vocabulary:

aatis *n.* artist

badlokid *adj.* unlucky

baffan *n.* clumsy person

craap *n., v.* scratch

faati leg *n.* millipede

farid *n.* forehead

jaah weh *v. phrase* pull away; move away

muo *adj., adv., pron.* more

PRACTICE EXERCISE 14

Translate the following sentences to Jamaican Creole.

1. They don't have enough money, so they will not go on the trip.
2. We won't go to the show.
3. They didn't expect to find the books.
4. He wouldn't pay her for the tickets.
5. John did not expect to pass the exam.
6. I do not believe they want us here.
7. She never wanted to get a cat.
8. The children will not take the exam because they are unprepared.
9. Carla was not in the office on Monday.
10. He sees nobody around, but it does not mean he is alone.

Translate the following sentences to English.

1. Wi neva decide when wi a goh staat di projek.
2. Peter noh wau none a dem fi nuo.
3. Alicia neva did nuo aar faada.
4. Yuh noh wau fi miss di laas paat a di movie.
5. Dem naah goh iht dinna till lyet inna di iivlin.
6. Di banana dem neva deh inna di dish.
7. Di pikni noh goh a school.
8. Ih naah goh en til dem goh weh.
9. George neva did andastan weh iih fi duh.
10. Di laaya noh deh inna di affis, soh iih seh wi noffi come tudeh.

Lesson Fifteen

Asking Questions

In English, there are a few ways to ask a question. An adverb (such as *where, when, how, why,* etc.), a pronoun (such as *who* or *whose*), a modal auxiliary verb (such as *can, will,* etc.), or the verb *be* is used to begin the sentence. An example is *Where is he?* In Jamaican Creole, questions are structured like statements. For example:

Jamaican Creole	English
Who deh ya?	Who is here?
*How dem nuo?	lit. How they know? (*How do they know?*)
Dem can dwiit?	lit. They can do it? (*Can they do it?*)

*Note that when the verb *duh* would act as an auxiliary verb in the present tense, it is omitted (e.g., *Yuh nuo?* (*E. Do you know?*)).

The Verb Bi

In English, the verb *be* is used in some cases to begin a question. An example is *Are you a nurse?* In Jamaican Creole, the subject always comes before the verb as if one were making a statement (except in a few cases which will be discussed later). For example:

Jamaican Creole	*English*
Yuh <u>did a</u> di nurse?	lit. You <u>were</u> the nurse? (*Were you the nurse?*)
Im <u>did a</u> yuh fren?	lit. He <u>was</u> your friend? (*Was he your friend?*)
Dem <u>a plan fi lef</u>?	lit. They <u>are planning to leave</u>? (*Are they planning to leave?*)

Remember from previous lessons that the verb *bi* is conjugated *deh* when it indicates location or position. The verb is also conjugated *deh* when the whereabouts of the subject is being inquired about. For example:

Jamaican Creole	*English*
Weh iih <u>deh</u>?	lit. Where he <u>is</u>? (*Where is he?*)
Wichpaat di book dem <u>did deh</u>?	lit. Where the books <u>had been</u>? (*Where had the books been?*)
How im did nuo seh dem <u>neva did dideh</u>?	lit. How he did know that they <u>had not been</u> there? (*How did he know that they had not been there?*)

Note that *deh* is sometimes omitted when the location or position of a noun is being inquired about in the simple present tense: example 1. *Weh yuh madda?* (E. *Where is your mother?*); example 2. *Weh dem girl?* (E. *Where are the/those girls?*). Note that *deh* is **not** omitted when the location or position of a pronoun is being inquired about. An example of this is *Weh shi deh?* (E. lit. *Where she is?/Where is she?*).

When an adjective is used in direct association with the verb *bi* in a sentence, the verb is conjugated based on the tense being used (*Review tenses if necessary*). For example:

Jamaican Creole	English
Di winda <u>neva</u> opin?	The window <u>wasn't</u> open?
Maria <u>did</u> sick?	Maria <u>was</u> sick?
Di sky cloudy?	The sky <u>is</u> cloudy?

When an adverb such as *weh* (E. *where*), *wichpaat* (E. *where*), *wishpaat* (E. *where*), *wyer* (E. *where*), E. *when*, E. *how*, E. *why*, *wa* (E. *what*), or E. *which*, or a pronoun such as E. *who, fuu* (E. *whose*), or *fihuu* (E. *whose*) is used to inquire about the subject of the sentence (except when the location or position of the subject is being inquired about), the verb can be:

1. used in the base infinitive form, *bi*. In this case, the subject and the object of the sentence are placed before the verb. For example:

Jamaican Creole	English
Who dat <u>did bi</u>?	lit. Who that <u>was</u>? (*Who was that?*)
Fuu demya <u>bi</u>?	lit. Whose these <u>are</u>? (*Whose are these?*)
Wa dis <u>bi</u>?	lit. What this <u>is</u>? (*What is this?*)

2. omitted from the sentence altogether if one is utilizing the simple present tense. For example:

Jamaican Creole	English
Who dat?	Who <u>is</u> that?
Fuu demya?	Whose <u>are</u> these?
Wa dis?	What <u>is</u> this?

Note *that rule 2* does not apply when *ih* or *it* is used before or after the verb. In these cases, *rule 1* or *rule 3* is followed. An example of the correct usage is *Wa ih bi?* (lit. *What it is?*/E. *What is it?*).

3. or is conjugated *a* or *a did* (also used as *a beeh, a weeh, a beeh did*, or *a weeh did*) and is used at the beginning of the sentence. For example:

Jamaican Creole	English
<u>A did</u> who dat?	lit. <u>It was</u> who that? (*Who was that?*)
<u>A</u> fuu demya?	lit. <u>It is</u> whose these? *Whose are these?*)
<u>A</u> wa dis?	lit. <u>It is</u> what this? (*What is this?*)

Sometimes Jamaicans add a redundant *a* at the beginning of questions. This is mainly done for emphasis or merely out of habit. It would seem like a version of the passive voice. For example:

Jamaican Creole	English
<u>A</u> who did seh dat?	lit. <u>It was</u> who had said that? (*Who had said that?*)
<u>A</u> weh im deh?	lit. <u>It is</u> where he is? (*Where is he?*)
<u>A</u> when dem a come?	lit. <u>It is</u> when they are coming? (*When are they coming?*)

Build Your Jamaican Creole Vocabulary:

baak *n., v.* bark

croffish *adj.* lacking ambition; lazy

dashweh *v. phrase* throw away; spill

gaa *contr.* go to

paach *v.* parch

ragga-ragga *adj., v.* untidy (regards clothing)

tompa *adj.* stocky

washi *adj.* weak

PRACTICE EXERCISE 15

Translate the following questions to Jamaican Creole.

1. Where did they put the box with the old pictures?
2. Which bus can I take from Downtown Kingston to Crossroads?
3. How many students are in the class?
4. Are they still leaving for Mexico next week?
5. Who is it?
6. When are we leaving for the show?
7. What happened to my new dress?
8. Where did you go for vacation last year?
9. How are they planning to do it?
10. Is she not going?

Translate the following sentences to English.

1. A weh dem a goh?
2. A which one a dem did win di trophy?
3. How much a dem lef?
4. A when a di laas dyeh fi fill out di application?
5. Who mash-op di TV?
6. When a di laas time yuh feed di cat an di daag?
7. A who lef di suoda opin pan di tyeb'l?
8. Wa a di bes wyeh fi study fi di final exam?
9. Wamek yuh noh finish disya projek bifuo yuh staat di adda one?
10. Weh dem did deh when wi did a duh all a di wok?

Lesson Sixteen

Showing Ownership

The methods for showing ownership in English and Jamaican Creole are very similar. A discussion of possessive pronouns, adjectives demonstrating possession, and possessive nouns follows.

The Possessive Pronouns

The following possessive pronouns are used to show ownership in both English and Jamaican Creole.

Table 7: Possessive Pronouns

Person	*Jamaican Creole*	*English*
First (sing.)	fimmi	mine
Second (sing.)	fiyuh	yours
Third (sing.)	fihim	his
	fiar	hers
	fiit/fihit	its
First (plur.)	fiwi	ours
Second (plur.)	fiunnu/fuunu	yours
Third (plur.)	fidem	theirs

101

The possessive pronouns of Jamaican Creole are used in the same way as they are in English. For example:

Jamaican Creole	English
Di purple bag a <u>fimmi</u>.	The purple bag is <u>mine</u>.
Di house a <u>fidem</u>.	The house is <u>theirs</u>.
A <u>fiunnu</u>.	It is <u>yours</u>.

Uon (E. *own*) is sometimes used along with the possessive pronoun to indicate ownership. For example:

Jamaican Creole	English
A <u>fimmi uon</u>.	lit. It is <u>mine own</u>. (*It is mine*).
Dem a <u>fihim uon</u>.	lit. They are <u>his own</u>. (*They are his*).
Di kyaar a <u>fiar uon</u>.	lit. The car is <u>hers own</u>. (*The car is hers*).

Adjectives Demonstrating Possession

The possessive adjectives are used in the same way as they are in English.

Table 8: Possessive Adjectives

Person	Jamaican Creole	English
First (sing.)	mi/fimmi	my
Second (sing.)	yuh/fiyuh	your
Third (sing.)	iih/im/fihim	his
	aar/fiar	her
	ih/fiit/fihit	its
First (plur.)	wi/fiwi	our
Second (plur.)	unnu/fiunnu/fuunu	your
Third (plur.)	deeh/dem/fidem	their

Examples of the possessive adjectives:

Jamaican Creole	*English*
A <u>fimmi bicycle</u>.	It is <u>my bicycle</u>.
<u>Ih tyel</u> brok.	<u>Its tail</u> is broken.
A <u>unnu madda</u> did seh soh.	It is <u>your mother</u> [who] had said so.

It is important to note that possessive adjectives that begin with *fi* (such as *fimmi, fiyuh, fihim,* etc.) are more emphatic or demonstrate a stronger connection to the thing possessed than do the others (such as *mi, yuh, im,* etc.). This is especially true if one is demonstrating how one is related to, or how one is associated with, another person. So, if one were to say *A mi anti* (E. *It is my aunt*), the level of possessiveness is lower or less emphatic than if one were to say *A fimmi anti*.

The Possessive Nouns

In English, ownership is communicated by adding *'s* or *'* to the noun. Examples include *the girls' heads* and *Shawn's dog*. In Jamaican Creole, there are three ways to show ownership over a noun:

1. No addition is made to the noun. The two nouns are merely stated one behind the other, and it is understood that the first mentioned noun owns the second. For example:

Jamaican Creole	*English*
Di <u>uhman daag</u> dig wau huol inna di yaad laas week.	The <u>woman's dog</u> dug a hole in the yard last week.
<u>Trudy bwuayfren</u> pick aar up every dyeh.	<u>Trudy's boyfriend</u> picks her up every day.
<u>Peter money</u> laas.	<u>Peter's money</u> is lost.

2. *A fi* is used before the noun to mean *is for* or *are for*. For example:

Jamaican Creole	English
A fi Sharlene.	lit. It <u>is for</u> Sharlene. *(It is Sharlene's).*
Di buon <u>a fi</u> di daag.	lit. The bone <u>is for</u> the dog. *(It is the dog's bone).*
Di book dem <u>a fi</u> di school.	lit. The books <u>are for</u> the school. *(The books are the school's).*

3. *Uon* is placed after the noun. For example:

Jamaican Creole	English
A <u>Sharlene uon</u>.	lit. It is <u>Sharlene's own</u>. *(It is Sharlene's).*
It a di <u>daag uon</u>.	lit. It is the <u>dog's own</u>. *(It is the dog's).*
Dem a di <u>school uon</u>.	lit. They are the <u>school's own</u>. *(They are the school's).*

Sometimes there is a combination of formations 2 and 3 above. An example is *A fi Sharlene uon* (E. *It is Sharlene's*).

Build Your Jamaican Creole Vocabulary:

aan *adv.* on

bengereng *n.* anything excessively ornate, shabby, or old.

grong *n.* field; farm; ground

kaapet/kyaapet *n., v.* carpet

piini/piini walli *n.* firefly

red-yai *adj., n.* envious; envy

sih'n *adv., pron., n.* thing; something

taiyad *adj., v.* tired; tire

PRACTICE EXERCISE 16

Translate the following sentences to Jamaican Creole.

1. My mother's friend is my teacher.
2. Carl's wife does not like his friends because she thinks that they are a bad influence.
3. One of the dog's toys is on the lawn.
4. It is our right to do as we please.
5. The farm is theirs.
6. A portion of the river is John's since it flows across his land.
7. Her father decided not to let her go to the dance.
8. Julie's parrot flew out the window.
9. The dress that I wore to the ball was Jana's.
10. Their team won the championship.

Translate the following sentences to English.

1. Di man foot deh pan di tyeb'l.
2. Di girl pull out wau makka out a di daag paw.
3. Shawna fren neva goh wid aar.
4. Deeh company put aan wau big paati fi di employee dem.
5. All a di arinj tree dem deh pau Maas Joe lan.
6. Timmy madda neva deh a di meeting.
7. All a di profit a fiwi uon.
8. When shi hyeh seh aar fren did win, shi cud'n believe ih.
9. Diane letta neva reach til yessideh.
10. Fihim kyaar a di red one.

Lesson Seventeen

Forming Adjectives And Adverbs

Adjectives

Adjectives are used similarly in English and in Jamaican Creole. You will remember from previous lessons that the verb *bi* behaves irregularly before adjectives and is usually omitted before them. Small differences, however, exist with the use of adjectives in English and the use of adjectives in Jamaican Creole:

1. Jamaicans sometimes repeat adjectives for emphasis. This is true of adjectives that describe emotions or moods. For example:

Jamaican Creole	*English*
Shi <u>upset upset</u> oova it.	She is [very] <u>upset</u> over it.
Im did <u>sad sad</u>.	He was [very] <u>sad</u>.
Shelly <u>sick sick</u> wid di flu.	Shelly is [very] <u>sick</u> with the flu.

Certain adjectives (for e.g., *fenkeh-fenkeh* (E. *weak*), *likki-likki* (E. *greedy*), and *nyami-nyami* (E. *greedy*)) are adjectives that have a 'dependence' on repetition. This means that if used singly, the word would be meaningless. This can be termed a 'dependent repetition.' The repetition of the word is also not a function of emotion or mood, nor is it being repeated for emphasis.

2. Consistent with the present perfect and past perfect tenses in Jamaican Creole, words that require *ed* to form their adjectives in English (e.g. determined) generally remain unchanged in Jamaican Creole. For example:

Jamaican Creole	*English*
Tim a di <u>muo determine</u> one.	Tim is the <u>more determined</u> one.
Im <u>position</u> a di front.	He is <u>positioned</u> at the front.
Wi live inna wau <u>develop</u> iyeria.	We live in a <u>developed</u> area.

3. Generally speaking, **comparative adjectives** are used similarly in Jamaican Creole and in English. In English, the **comparative degree** is used when comparing two people or things, and *er* or *more* is used with the adjective to form the comparative degree. The **superlative degree** is used when comparing more than two people or things, and *est* or *most* is used with the adjective to form the superlative degree.

   The comparative and superlative degrees in Jamaican Creole are formed as in English, except that *a* is used in place of *er*, and *muo* is used in place of *more* for the comparative degree. For the superlative degree, *is* or *es* is used instead of *est*, and *muos* is used instead of *most*. The rules governing the use of the comparative degree and the superlative degree are not as strict as in English. As such, you will find that people will use the comparative degree or superlative degree to compare two people or things or more than two people or things.

Examples Of Comparative Degree

Jamaican Creole	*English*
Jack <u>faasa</u> dan Fred.	Jack is <u>faster</u> than Fred.
Jane a wau <u>betta</u> sumaddi dau Jim.	Jane is a <u>better</u> person than Jim.
Di red van <u>bigga</u> dan di blue one.	The red van is <u>bigger</u> than the blue one.

The comparative adjectives that are irregular in English are also irregular in Jamaican Creole. They include:

JC.	bad	wos	wos
E.	bad	worse	worst
JC.	good	betta	bes
E.	good	better	best
JC.	likk'l	less	liis
E.	little	less	least
JC.	many	muo	muos
E.	many	more	most
JC.	much	muo	muos
E.	much	more	most

Examples Of Superlative Degree

Jamaican Creole	*English*
Tim a di <u>muos determine</u> one out a all a dem.	Tim is the <u>most determined</u> one out of all of them.
Out a di three a dem, Toni a di <u>bes</u>.	Out of the three of them, Toni is the <u>best</u>.
Out of the ten classroom dem, dis one a di <u>naiziis</u>.	Out of the ten classrooms, this one is the <u>noisiest</u>.

Adverbs

There are slight differences in the use of adverbs in Jamaican Creole and the use of adverbs in English. Those adverbs that end in –*ly* in English are usually used without the –ly in Jamaican Creole. For example:

Jamaican Creole	*English*
*Shi did ak <u>bryev</u> when di tiif attack aar.	She acted <u>bravely</u> when the thief attacked her.
Shi did tell im <u>plyen</u>.	She told him <u>plainly</u>.
Deeh walk <u>sluo</u>.	They walk <u>slowly</u>.

*This sentence can also connote the idea that the person is pretending to be brave.

Jamaicans have a tendency to repeat an adverb for emphasis. This is especially true when an action is being communicated to have taken place in some extraordinary manner. For example:

Jamaican Creole	*English*
Wi did reach Ocho Rios <u>faas faas</u>.	We reached Ocho Rios [very] <u>fast</u>.
Di line a move <u>sluo sluo</u>.	The line is moving [very] <u>slowly</u>.
Iih seh it <u>plyen plyen</u>.	He said it [very] <u>plainly</u>.

Jamaicans sometimes avoid forming adverbs in sentences. Instead, they opt to construct the sentence in such a way that it does not require an adverb. For example:

Instead Of Saying:	*One Might Say:*	
English	*Jamaican Creole*	*English Translation*
The children chat noisily.	Di pikni dem naizi.	The children are noisy.
Something is terribly wrong.	So'mn wrong, man.	Something is wrong, man.
He accepted it happily.	Iih did happy fi aksep ih.	He was happy to accept it.

Comparing Adverbs

The **comparative degree** in English is usually formed by adding *er* or using *more* with the adverb. In Jamaican Creole, the comparative degree is formed by adding *a* or using *muo*. Sometimes the comparative degree in Jamaican Creole that is formed by *a* is used in place of the one formed by *muo*. For example:

Instead Of Saying:	*One Might Say:*
English	*Jamaican Creole*
He reacted <u>more quickly</u> than the other runners.	Iih riak <u>quicka</u> dan di adda runna dem.
I see it <u>more clearly</u> now.	Mi siit <u>cleara</u> now.
The car is moving <u>more slowly</u> than the bus.	Di kyaar a move <u>slowa</u> dan the bus.

The **superlative degree** in English typically has the ending *est*. In Jamaican Creole, it is formed by adding *is* or *es* to the adverb. The superlative degree that is formed by adding *most* in English is **not** used in Jamaican Creole. You are unlikely to hear a Jamaican say, for example, *Shi sing out muos happily* (E. *She sings out most happily*), unless they are speaking English. For example:

Jamaican Creole	*English*
Dem did come ya di <u>earliis</u>.	They came here the <u>earliest</u>.
Di yellow one laas <u>langes</u>.	The yellow one lasts <u>longest</u>.
Wi wi si who run <u>faases</u>.	We will see who runs <u>fastest</u>.

The comparative adverbs that are irregular in English are also irregular in Jamaican Creole. They include:

JC.	bad	wos	wos
E.	badly	worse	worst

JC.	far	fara	fares
E.	far	farther	farthest

JC.	lyet	lyeta	laas
E.	late	later	last

JC.	much	muo	muos
E.	much	more	most

JC.	well	betta	bes
E.	well	better	best

Build Your Jamaican Creole Vocabulary:

baan *adj.* born
chrip *v.* strip
en *n., v.* end
haad *adj., adv.* hard

noh'n *adv., n.* nothing
ramp *v.* play
sooweh *adv.* somewhere
waa/wa a *contr.* what is

PRACTICE EXERCISE 17

Translate the following sentences to Jamaican Creole.

1. James is more studious than George.
2. The man walked slowly down the street.
3. Mr. Johnson is the best teacher in the school.
4. Sara is the funniest person I know.
5. She walked more quickly to the shop than usual.
6. I am better at English than I am at Spanish.
7. He knows the governor really well.
8. Heather danced more gracefully than her friend.
9. The radio was playing loudly when they came home.
10. She is the nicer of the two sisters.

Translate the following sentences to English.

1. Jessica muo ambitious dau Tim.
2. Mr. Brown a di bes tiicha mi ha.
3. Iih drive faasa dan dat.
4. John finish iih wok quick.
5. Mi tink Suzie inna wau betta position fi mek wau decision bout di situation dau di manija.
6. Di bwuay shout out loud.
7. Di kyaar climb di hill steady.
8. Out a di two a dem, im a di wos.
9. Di ol man a di happies sumaddi mi kyah tink a.
10. Wi wyet pyeshent pau dem fi a long time.

Lesson Eighteen

Da, Datdeh, Dat, Seh, And Weh

Thereare five words in Jamaican Creole whose meanings trans-late to *that* in English. They are *da, datdeh, dat, seh*, and *weh*.

Da

Da is used only as an adjective that is followed by a noun: e.g., *Shi look like da uhman pau TV* (E. *She looks like that woman on TV*). It can be used to point out a noun somewhere in the distance: e.g., *Yuh si da girl oova dehsoh?* (E. *You see that girl over there?*). *Deh* (E. *there*), *dyer* (E. *there*), *dehsoh* (E. *there/right there*), and *dyersoh* (E. *there/right there*) are frequently added after the noun referred to by *da* to indicate the specific location of the subject: e.g., *Yuh si da girl deh oova dehsoh?* (E. *You see that girl there over there?*).

Datdeh

Datdeh identifies a thing, although it can be used in an offensive way as a pronoun to refer to a person. It is used as an adjective or pronoun. It is **not**, however, used as a relative pronoun that is equivalent to which or who (such as *letter that she sent him*). *Deh* (E. *there*), *dyer* (E. *there*), *dehsoh* (E. *there/right there*), and *dyersoh* (E. *there/right there*) are frequently added after the noun referred to by *datdeh* to indicate the specific location of the subject. Examples of how *datdeh* is used:

Jamaican Creole	English
Datdeh bag deh a fimmi.	That bag there is mine.
A wa datdeh?	lit. It is what that? (*What is that?*)
Gi mi datdeh.	Give me that.

Dat

Dat is used interchangeably with E. *that* as an adjective, adverb, conjunction, and pronoun. It can also be used in an offensive manner as a pronoun to refer to a person. When used as an adjective, *deh* (E. *there*), *dyer* (E. *there*), *dehsoh* (E. *there/right there*), and *dyersoh* (E. *there/right there*) are frequently added after the noun being referred to by *dat* to indicate the specific location of the subject: e.g., *Dat bag dyer a fihim* (E. *That bag there is his*). Examples of the use of *dat*:

Jamaican Creole	English
Ih did soh hat dat mi tek aaf mi shot.	It was so hot that I took off my shirt.
Deeh gi soh dat deeh kyah receive.	They give so that they can receive.
Shi duh dat.	She does that.

Seh

Seh is used as a conjunction. It is used after a clause expressing fact, belief, wish, hope, expectation, opinion, decision, or some feeling/emotion: e.g., *Wi nuo seh iih did win wau prize* (E. *We knew that he won a prize*). Note, when the verb *seh* (E. *say*) is used before the conjunction *seh*, the conjunction is omitted. An example of this is *Shi did seh im a fool* (E. *She had said that he is a fool*).

Weh

Weh is used as a relative pronoun that is equivalent to *which* or *who* in usage. For example:

> JC. Shi deh pan di committee <u>weh</u> deal wid scholarship.
> E. She is on the committee <u>that</u> deals with scholarships.

Whenever you are doubtful about which one of the above words to use, it is always safe to use *dat*.

Build Your Jamaican Creole Vocabulary:

bakk'l *n., v.* bottle

hoks *n., v.* hack; husk

kaad *n.* cord

lakka dat *adv.* like that

naiz *n.* noise

obyeh *v.* obey

pakit *adj., n., v.* pocket

ruop *n., v.* rope

PRACTICE EXERCISE 18

Translate the following sentences to Jamaican Creole.

1. I hope that everything will be alright.
2. That is the first time I have ever heard him say that.
3. The best thing that you can do is to ignore his comments.
4. Is it true that you are planning to leave the country in a month?
5. That day was most memorable.
6. If you give me something that I want, I will give you something that you want.
7. That house right there is where we used to live.
8. He thinks it is your fault that the cat ran away.
9. It is funny that she turned out to be your aunt's friend.
10. Is that Janice?

Translate the following sentences to English.

1. Iih noh andastan seh wi haffi lef now?
2. Dat a di one weh shi did a talk bout.
3. Datdeh sumaddi weh sen di gif nice.
4. Da man deh did jos a aks mi fi John.
5. Deeh did tell mi seh mi noh ha nof time lef pan di exam.
6. Dat true.
7. All a di money weh wi spen a fi noh'n.
8. Dat a all wi ha lef?
9. Mi did soh mizareb'l dat mi neva badda styeh.
10. All di people dem weh did deh pan di buot syev.

Lesson Ninteen

The Tendency To Use Goh And Come After Verbs Of Movement

Goh and E. *come* are sometimes used after verbs that demonstrate movement (e.g., *walk*, *run*, *ride*, *fly,* and *send*). This verb formation connotes the idea that the action leads to some place close (*come*) to the speaker or subject, some place at a distance (*goh*) from the speaker or subject, or from one place to another, depending on the direction of the movement. They should only be used if that is the idea the speaker wishes to convey. For example:

Jamaican Creole	*English*
Shi <u>did run goh</u> a di bus stop.	lit. She <u>ran go</u> to the bus stop. (*She ran to the bus* stop).
Mi <u>naah walk goh</u> bikaah ih too far.	lit. I <u>am not walking go</u> because it's too far. (*I am not walking [to there] because it's too far*).
Wendy <u>a fly come</u> huom soon.	lit. Wendy <u>is flying come</u> home soon. (*Wendy is flying home soon*).

Sometimes there is a delay between the verb and its modifier. These are cases where a noun or pronoun (or a noun or pronoun phrase) occurs between the verb and *goh* or *come*. For example:

Jamaican Creole	*English*
Dem <u>a move</u> di store <u>come</u> a Montego Bay.	lit. They <u>are moving</u> the store <u>come</u> to Montego Bay. (*They are moving the store to Montego Bay*).
It <u>deh</u> pan di wyeh <u>goh</u> a Mandeville.	lit. It <u>is</u> on the way <u>go</u> to Mandeville. (*It is on the way to Mandeville*).
Di truck <u>carry</u> plank buod frau May Pen <u>goh</u> a town.	lit. The truck <u>carries</u> plank boards from May Pen <u>go</u> to town. (*The truck carries plank boards from May Pen to town*).

Sometimes *goh* or *come* will be conjugated instead of the main verb to indicate the tense of the sentence. For example:

Jamaican Creole	*English*
Dem <u>move</u> the store <u>a come</u> a Montego Bay.	lit. They <u>move</u> the store <u>is coming</u> to Montego Bay. (*They are moving the store to Montego Bay*).
Wi <u>deh</u> pan wi wyeh <u>did a goh</u> a di paati.	lit. We <u>are</u> on our way <u>were going</u> to the party. (*We were on our way to the party*).
Di truck <u>carry</u> plank buod frau May Pen <u>a goh</u> a town.	lit. The truck <u>carries</u> plank boards from May Pen <u>is going</u> to town. (*The truck is carrying plank boards from May Pen to town*).

Goh, cooh, and *come* are sometimes used before verbs to express surprise, annoyance, or disdain. In these instances, *goh, cooh,* and *come* are usually not indicating literal direction or location, although they sometimes do. The verbs they modify are not limited to verbs of movement. Usually, the action or event took place in the recent past. For example:

Jamaican Creole	English
Rachel <u>come tell</u> mi seh shi naah dwiit.	lit. Rachel <u>come tell</u> me that she is not doing it. (*Rachel told me that she is not doing it*).
John <u>cooh si</u> aar a spalding.	lit. John <u>come see</u> her in Spalding. (*John saw her in Spalding*).
Dem <u>come tek over</u>.	lit. They <u>come take over</u>. (*They took over*).

The Use Of Jump Goh, Jump Come, Jump Cooh, And Goh

Jump goh, jump come, jump cooh, or *goh* is often used before a verb to suggest that an action was done on a whim, without consideration, or without regard for another person's feelings. *Jump* is pronounced as in English. In most instances, the action or statement is inappropriate or invidious. These phrases most times do not indicate literal direction or physical location. For example:

Jamaican Creole	*English*
Shi <u>did jump goh dwiit</u>.	lit. She <u>jumped go do</u> it. (*She did it [on a whim/without much consideration]*).
Andy <u>jump come seh</u> shi fi lef di school.	lit. Andy <u>jump come say</u> she should leave the school. (*Andy said [on a whim] that she should leave the school*).
Mary <u>goh sign</u> aar nyem pan di pyepa.	lit. Mary <u>go sign</u> her name on the paper. (*Mary [inappropriately] signed her name on the paper*).
Pete <u>jump cooh feed</u> di daag, an now di daag sick.	lit. Pete <u>jump come feed</u> the dog, and now the dog is sick. (*Pete fed the dog, and now the dog is sick*).

Build Your Jamaican Creole Vocabulary:

ancaal-fa *adj.* uncalled-for

dochi *n.* small, round pot

higla *n.* peddler; vendor; a person who sells ground produce in a food market

likk'l-muo *inter.* later

maanin *interj., n.* morning

saadiin *n.* sardine

uov'n *n.* oven

wok *n., v.* work

PRACTICE EXERCISE 19

Try to decipher whether or not *goh, come, cooh, jump goh, jump come,* or *jump cooh* is required in the following sentences. Translate all sentences to Jamaican Creole.

1. We ran to the crossroads and then ran back to the house.
2. We drove to Montego Bay.
3. He took the bus from Mandeville to Kingston.
4. Joe went to the party, even though nobody invited him.
5. Odette flies to Japan every year.
6. She gave them information that they should not have.
7. It happened on the way from Manchester to St. Catherine.
8. They transport furniture to Spanish Town daily.
9. Ian will move to Mile Gully next month.
10. He ran to call for help.

Translate the following sentences to English.

1. Shi jump goh put aan wau new skirt fi impress im.
2. Joan an aar family travel goh a di festival every iyer.
3. Wi naah jaiv goh a Portland. Wi aggo tek ih bus.
4. Mi deh pan mi wyeh a goh a Charleston.
5. Yuh walk come huom tudeh?
6. Judy goh seh Charlene a wyes aar time, an Charlene upset now.
7. Wi cooh meet dem a di craasruod.
8. Shi run cooh giim ih bifuo iih lef.
9. Emily bring di glass come.
10. She did run goh dong deh fi mi.

Lesson Twenty

Commands

A command is an order. It indicates what someone should do. Commands begin with a verb, and this verb describes how the pronoun (*you*) should act upon another noun or pronoun (e.g., *Take it to her*). It is understood that *you* (pronoun) *take it* (pronoun that should be acted upon) *to her* (pronoun action is directed towards). Commands are used in Jamaican Creole as they are in English. For example:

Jamaican Creole	*English*
Put ih pan di tyeb'l.	Put it on the table.
Tek ih to im.	Take it to him.
Memba fi call.	Remember to call.

Commands Involving The Verb Gi

The verb *gi* is generally used in commands as it is in English. For example:

Jamaican Creole	English
<u>Gi</u> di pet to aar.	<u>Give</u> the pet to her.
<u>Giim</u> di bag fi huol.	<u>Give him</u> the bag to hold.
<u>Gimmi</u> mi watch.	<u>Give me</u> my watch.

The noun or pronoun that should be acted upon can be omitted if all parties are aware of what object/s should be acted upon. Look at the following examples:

Jamaican Creole	English
Giim.	Give [it/them to] him.
Gi aar.	Give [it/them to] her.
Gi dem.	Give [it/them to] them.
Gimmi.	Give [it/them to] me.

Sometimes when there are objects being acted upon (plural), *dem* is added at the end of the sentence to communicate this. Look at the following examples:

Jamaican Creole	English
Giim <u>dem</u>.	lit. Give him <u>them</u>. (*Give them to him*).
Gi aar <u>dem</u>.	lit. Give her <u>them</u>. (*Give them to her*).
Gi dem <u>dem</u>.	lit. Give them <u>them</u>. (*Give them to them*).
Gimmi <u>dem</u>.	lit. Give me <u>them</u>. (*Give them to me*).

Negative Commands

Noh, *dooh*, and *duo* are used in negative commands. They mean *do not (don't)*. For example:

Jamaican Creole	English
<u>Noh</u> put ih deh.	<u>Don't</u> put it there.
<u>Duo</u> goh wid im.	<u>Don't</u> go with him.
<u>Dooh</u> sisso.	<u>Don't</u> say so.

Negative, Compound Commands

When *noh*, *dooh*, and *duo* are used in compound sentences, both clauses require one of these negative auxiliaries. Any combination of the words can be used. For example:

Jamaican Creole	English
<u>Noh</u> giim di money, an <u>noh</u> tell im seh mi seh soh.	<u>Don't</u> give him the money, and <u>don't</u> tell him that I said so.
<u>Dooh</u> goh a Mandeville, an <u>duo</u> goh a May Pen.	<u>Don't</u> go to Mandeville, and <u>don't</u> go to May Pen.
<u>Duo</u> ak lakka seh mi neva tell yuh, an <u>noh</u> ak lakka seh yuh neva nuo.	<u>Don't</u> act like I did not tell you, and <u>don't</u> act like you did not know.

Repetition Of Nouns, Pronouns, And Verbs

It was discussed in *Lesson Seventeen* that adjectives and adverbs are sometimes repeated. Some nouns, pronouns, and verbs are also repeated. Nouns and verbs that are repeated can be 'repetition dependent' (e.g., *soc-soc* (E. *a frozen, flavored drink*) and *chakka-chakka* (E. *to mess up*)), or they are repeated for emphasis (e.g., *gyal gyal dem* (E. *girls* or *young women* [especially when the girls or young women are considered lazy, idle, ill-mannered, or uncultured]) and *dash dash di gyabij evriweh* (E. *throw the garbage everywhere*)).

Verbs are sometimes repeated to communicate that something was done in an extraordinary manner or happened repeatedly. *Op* is frequently added to these verbs (e.g., *maak maak-op di duo wid pencil* (E. *repeatedly marked the door with a pencil*)). Pronouns are sometimes repeated for emphasis. These pronouns allude to quantity or amount (e.g., *wau nof nof* (E. *want plenty/a lot*)).

The Use Of A And Fi

Two prepositions are used in Jamaican Creole to mean *to* in English. They are *a* and *fi*. The English word *to* is also used in Jamaican Creole, except in some of the instances below where *a* and *fi* are used.

The Use Of A

A is used to indicate:

1. direction or destination: e.g., *Di kyaar did a head a St. Mary* (E. *The car was heading to St. Mary*).
2. position of someone or something (though E. *to* is more frequently used): e.g., *Di bookshelf deh a di right a di door* (E. *The bookshelf is to the right of the door*).

The Use Of Fi

Fi is only used to form the infinitive of verbs: e.g., *Mi ha fi goh a Spalding tomorrow* (E. *I have to go to Spalding tomorrow*).

The Use Of Ku

Ku (E. *look*) is used in exclamations to draw attention to something or someone (otherwise E. *look* is used): e.g. 1. *Ku pau yuh!* (E. *Look at you!*); E.g. 2. *Ku pan da cat deh!* (E. *Look at that cat there!*)

The Use Of Fi And Fa

Fi and *fa* are used interchangeably. They both mean E. *for*. It should be noted, however, that *fi* is more frequently used. When *Fa* is used before *ih* or *it,* an *r* is added at the end of the word. An example is *Mi haffi goh look far ih* (E. *I have to go look for it*). When *fi* is used before *ih* or *it,* the two words are pronounced as if they were one word. An example is *Mi haffi goh fiit* (E. *I have to go for it*). *Fi* is **not** used at the end of a sentence. *Fa* is always used in this case. An example is *Weh yuh a goh fa?* (E. *What are you going for?*). This sentence can also mean *Why are you going?*

The Case Of Kyah And Kyaah

When spoken, it can be difficult to distinguish between the words *kyah* and *kyaah* (E. *can* and E. *cannot*). So how do you know when the speaker means that he or she can or cannot? Well, as is the case with some other words and ideas in Jamaican Creole, one has to pay attention to the broader context within which these words or ideas are being communicated.

In this specific case, one has to pay attention to the verbal and non-verbal cues that the person employs when saying these words. If the person says *no man*, frowns, gives a little headshake, or pronounces an elongated *aa* sound, it is very likely that the person is saying that he or she cannot. If, on the other hand, the person says *yes/yeh man*, gives a little nod, or pronounces a sharper *a* sound, it is very likely that the person is saying he or she can.

Gender

In Jamaican Creole, the masculine gender is sometimes used to refer to both genders. So, it is not uncommon to hear someone referring to a female as *iih, im, iihself, fihim,* etc. Normally, it is established whom is being spoken about by the mention of a name, or some other indication is given. In English, an animal or baby is referred to as *it.* In Jamaican Creole, a baby is either referred to by gender, or the masculine gender is used irrespective of actual gender (especially in rural parishes). An animal is more frequently referred to as the masculine gender *iih* and *im* (E. *he, his,* etc.), although the feminine gender is sometimes used to refer to a female animal.

Build Your Jamaican Creole Vocabulary:

ak *n., v.* act

iyez-jrom *n.* eardrum

likk'l-muos *adv.* almost

lyeh *n., v.* lay

maskita *n.* mosquito

pongkin *n.* pumpkin

ruobot *n., v.* robot; illegal taxi; taxi driver operating illegal taxi; to operate a taxi illegally

saiyans *n., v.* obeah

PRACTICE EXERCISE 20

Translate the following sentences to Jamaican Creole.

1. We are ready to leave.
2. Vacuum the carpet with the new vacuum cleaner.
3. Tell me where it is.
4. Give me one of your tickets.
5. Show me how to braid my hair.
6. Ask the receptionist to give you directions to Santa Cruz.
7. Let me know when you are ready.
8. Who is that for?
9. Send the package three days before his birthday.
10. Pick a suit for the wedding.

Lesson Twenty-One

Putting It All Together

Reading Comprehension 1

Di Laas Time Mi Did Goh A Beach

Di laas time mi goh a beach, a did wid mi family; mi madda, mi faada, mi granny, an mi bredda dem. Wi did goh a di Seven Miles Beach inna Negril. Di ride did lang auh taiyadin, auh wi cud'n reach faas enough fi mi. Daddy did tek wa iih call 'di scenic route,' an dat mean seh wi bypass di haiwyeh an drive pan nof bakka-bush, bad ruod. Wau good ting bout di ride a did seh wi tap fi buy sooh fruit frau sooh venda weh sell pan di ruodsaid. Granny did seh ih wudda bi betta if wi did goh a wau beach inna Portland, bikaah a dehsoh wi live. Dat a did di fos time mi a goh a datdeh beach deh. A did lakka noh'n mi eva si; mile pau tap a mile a white sand beach. Mi neva si noh'n soh pretty.

Mi bredda dem did excited, an deeh wud'n tap talk. All di wyeh goh a di beach dem jos a talk an talk. Ih neva jos tap a pretty iida. Di waata did cool auh nice, an di sun did waam tuh. Nof people did dideh, but dat did ong'l mek ih muo fun. Wi plyeh 'yuh a it' inna di waata wid some a di adda people dem, an mi ride pan di jetski wid mi faada an mi bredda dem. Dat did a nof fun! Mi jap aaf inna di waata two time, aalduo mi did fryed di fos time ih did ha'mn. Mi madda an mi granny did fryed fi try ih, soh dem sidong pan di san auh mek lunch. Fi lunch wi ha ackee, saalfish, an fry bammy. Dat did tyes good. Mi iht aaf all a fimmi an did wau muo, but mi bredda dem already finish fidem bifuo mi cudda goh haafwyeh chruu fimmi. Mi madda seh nex time shi wi mek sure fi put extra food inna di lunch bag. Afta lunch, wi goh pan di glass battam buot. Di ride did a nof fun tuh. Iiv'n Granny auh mommy try ih.

Things To Consider:

1. From whose perspective was the story told?
2. What were the main ideas of the passage?
3. Who were the people in the story?
4. Why did they go to the beach?
5. What happened while they were at the beach?
6. Were you able to translate the entire passage?
7. Did you recognize the different tenses used?

Reading Comprehension 2

Maas Deacon, Di Faama

Faama Deacon love di sumell a di dot, especially early inna di maanin. Dis maanin im love ih muo dau all di adda maanin dem bikaah a did time fi reap di yam dem weh iih plant aalmuos one iyer agoh. Iih dress inna iih usual uol khaki shot auh pants auh iht wau good byekfaas a callaluu an saalfish wid fry dumpling soh im kyah ha enough stamina fi di dyeh ahead. Iih pick up iih tool dem frau di shed and di likk'l dish a lunch weh did lef oova frau yessideh. Faama Deacon fling iih huo, cotlas, an iih faak oova iih shuolda. Im grab iih lunch inna iih free han auh staat pan im wyeh. Im seh 'maanin' to di likk'l pikini weh pass im pan aar wyeh a goh a school. Im craas di ruod an staat dong di track weh tek im to di sumaal grong inna di migg'l a wau fiil.

Di ruod did wet frau night dew, but Faama Deacon use to it by now. Afta all, a di syem ruod iih walk pan aalmuos every dyeh goh a grong. Di guava tree pan di side a di ruod ha nof guava pan ih. Aalduo iih iiga fi staat reap iih yam dem, iih stap auh pudong iih tool dem inna di ruod. Im pick a few a di guava dem. Iih bite one a dem an ih sweet like di star apple dem weh inna iih backyaad. Im pick as many as iih pakit cudda huol, an den im pick up iih tool dem an resume iih journey.

Pan di wyeh, Faama Deacon haffi pass wau spring weh run craas di ruod. Im nuo now seh iih very cluos to iih grong. Fi di sekan time, iih tek aaf iih bûrd'n an put ih pan di groun. Im squat dong beside di riva an wash im han dem weh get dotti from im tool dem. Im use im two han dem fi mek wau scoop and scoop up some a di waata fi drink. The waata cool auh nice, an ih always mek im feel refresh auh clean. Fi di laas time, im tek up im tool dem an staat di journey agen. By di time Faama Deacon reach iih grong, im a sweat bad. Iih drop di tool dem an carry di likk'l lunch goh put ih inna di hut weh im bil a di foot a di grong.

Things To Consider:

1. Who is Faama Deacon?
2. What did Faama Deacon set out to do?
3. Did Faama Deacon accomplish what he set out to do?
4. Were you able to translate the entire passage?
5. Did you recognize the different tenses used?

Frequently Asked Questions

Asking About Time

Ho much a clak?	lit. How much is clock? (*What time is it?*)
Wa time?	lit. What time? (*What time is it?*)
Wa time wi a lef?	lit. What time we are leaving? (*At what time are we leaving?*)
Wa time yuh ha?	lit. What time you have? (*What time do you have?*)
Yuh nuo a wa time?	lit. You know it is what time? (*Do you know what time it is?*)

Asking How Much Something Costs

A ho much dis/dat kaas?	lit. It is how much this/that costs? (*How much does this/that cost?*)
A ho much fi dis/dat?	lit. It is how much for this/that? (*How much is it for this/that?*)
Ho much dis/dat kaas?	lit. How much this/that costs? (*How much does this/that cost?*)
Ho much fi dis/dat?	lit. How much for this/that? (*How much is it for this/that?*)
Wa a di kaas a dis/dat?	What is the cost of this/that?

Asking About Location Of Places, Things, Or People

Weh di puos affis deh?	lit. Where the post office is? (*Where is the post office?*)
Weh mi kyah fain wau cambio?	lit. Where I can find a cambio? (*Where can I find a cambio?*)
Weh yuh deh?	lit. Where you are? (*Where are you?*)
Weh yuh from?	lit. Where you from? (*Where are you from?*)
Yuh kyah tell mi how fi reach...?	lit. You can tell me how to reach...? (*Can you tell me how to get to...?*)

General Questions

A wa?	lit. It is what? (*What is it?/What's the matter?*)
Noh true?	lit. No true? (*Isn't that true/ Isn't that so?*)
Waa gwaan?	lit. What's going on? (*What's up?/What's going on?*)
Wa/weh yuh a duh?	lit. What you are doing? (*What are you doing?*)
Wa/weh yuh deh pan?	lit. What you are on? (*What are you up to/What are you doing?*)
Weh yuh nyem?	lit. What you name? (*What is your name?/What are you named?*)
Who dat/datdeh?	lit. Who that? (*Who is that?*)

Commonly Used Expressions

A good.	lit. It is good (usually used with irony to mean: *serves you right*).
A soh dem tan.	lit. It is how they stay. (*That is how they are (characteristically)*).
A soh di ting set up.	lit. It is how the thing is set up. (*That's how life is.*)
Come ya, man.	Come here, man.
Cool noh, man.	lit. Cool no, man. (*Chill out, man.*)
Evriting kris.	lit. Everything ok. (*Everything is ok.*)
Ku deh.	lit. Look there. (*Look at that.*)
Ku pau yuh.	lit. Look on you. (*Look at you.*)
Ku ya.	lit. Look here. (*Look at this.*)
Kum-out.	Come out (can also mean: *get out*).
Main deh.	lit. Mind there. (*Move away from there/Be careful.*)
Mi come frau...	lit. I come from... (*I am from...*)
Mi dideh.	lit. I am there (can also mean: *I will be there.*)
Mi gone.	lit. I gone. (*I'm gone/Goodbye.*)
Mi naah lie yuh.	lit. I am not lying you. (*I'm not lying to you.*)

Mi nyem...	lit. My name... (*My name is...*)
Mi saat out.	lit. I sort out. (*I am doing good/doing ok.*)
Mi wi link yuh.	lit. I will link you. (*I will link up with you [at a later date/ time].*)
No problem, man.	(Although not Jamaican Creole, it is very commonly used in Jamaica.)
Put ih up.	lit. Put it up. (*Put it away for the future.*)
Right ya now.	lit. Right here now. (*Right now/At this moment.*)
Saat ih out/ Saat out...	lit. Sort it out/Sort out. (*Get it done.*)
Yeh, man.	Yes, man.
Yuh done nuo.	lit. You done know. (*You know it/You already know.*)
Yuh lucky.	lit. You lucky. (*You are lucky.*) (Used with irony to mean: *That is your misfortune/You deserve whatever misfor- tune befell you.*)
Yuh siit?	lit. You see it? (*You see what it is I'm saying?*)
Yuh si mi?	lit. You see me? (*You see what it is I'm saying?*)
Yuh ziit?	lit. You see it? (*You see what it is I'm saying?*)
Yuh zi mi?	lit. You see me? (*You see what it is I'm saying?*)

Frequently Used Jamaican Proverbs

As with English proverbs, the syntax of proverbs in Jamaican Creole is not necessarily used in everyday conversations. Words in parentheses are inserted for better understanding of the proverb.

Jamaican Proverb	Translation
Anno syem dyeh leaf jap inna waata ih ra'n.	It is not same day [that] leaf drops in water it [will] rot.
Bad luck wos dau obya.	Bad luck [is] worse than obeah. *(Obeah is a belief system that involves rituals and curses, much like witchcraft and voodoo.)*
Chicken merry, hawk deh near.	Chicken [is] merry, [but] hawk is near.
Cockroach noh bizniz inna fowl fight.	Cockroach [has] no business in fowl fight.
Cowad man kip soun buon.	[a] Coward man keeps sound bones.
Doppi nuo who fi frai'n.	[a] Ghost knows who to frighten.
Every mikk'l mek a mokk'l.	Every bit makes a lot.
Fos laugh anno laugh.	First laugh is not laugh. *(Its always best to have the last laugh.)*
Fowl weh feed a yaad easy fi ketch.	Fowl that feeds at [a] home is easy to catch.
Hag seh di fos waata yuh si, yuh wash.	Hog says the first water you see, you wash.
Hungry mek puss nyam paach caan.	Hunger makes puss eat parched corn.

Jamaican Proverb	*Translation*
If fish weh goh a riva battam tell yuh seh shaak dong deh, believe ih.	If fish that goes to river bottom tells you that shark is down there, believe it.
If yuh wau good, yuh nuoz haffi run.	If you want good, your nose has to run. *(If you want to achieve, you have to work hard.)*
Mi chuo mi caan; mi noh call noh fowl.	I threw my corn; I didn't call any fowls.
Noh chob'l chob'l till chob'l chob'l yuh.	Don't trouble trouble until trouble troubles you.
One, one cocoa, full baaskit.	One, one cocoa, full basket. *(Each cocoa helps to fill a basket.)*
Puss auh daag noh ha di syem luck.	Puss and dog do not have the same luck.
Wa noh dead, noh dashweh.	What is not dead, don't throw away.
Wa noh kill, fah'n; wa noh fah'n figah'n.	What doesn't kill, fattens; what doesn't fatten [is] forgotten.
Weh ih maaga, a deh ih pap.	Where it is slim, it is there it breaks.
Who kyaah hyeh aggo feel; finga mash, noh badda cry.	Who cannot hear will feel; finger mashed, don't bother [to] cry. *(If you refuse to listen to reason, you will suffer the consequences.)*

Appendix

Tenses Of Jamaican Creole Verbs

Verbs	Present Tense
aada *order*	aada
aks *ask*	aks
ansa *answer*	ansa
baak *bark*	baak
barro *borrow*	barro
bi *be*	a; deh; bi
brok *break*	brok
byed *bathe*	byed
chaaj *charge*	chaaj
chaka-chaka *mess up*	chaka-chaka
chrech *stretch*	chrech
chuo *throw*	chuo
dash-weh *throw away*	dash-weh
distraah *destroy*	distraah

duh *do*	duh
enta *enter*	enta
expek *expect*	expek
faam *farm*	faam
figet *forget*	figet
fren-op *make up with;* *make oneself friendly to*	fren-op
gi *give*	gi
goh *go*	goh
ha *have*	ha
hag-op *handle roughly;* *speak harshly to*	hag-op
hoks *hack; husk*	hoks
infek *infect*	infek
iyem *aim*	iyem
jaah *draw; pull*	jaah
juk *prick*	juk
ketch *catch*	ketch
konk *hit with sharp blow*	konk
laas *lose*	laas
laba *talk excessively*	laba
lef *leave*	lef
maach *march*	maach
myel *mail*	myel
nyem *name*	nyem
opin *open*	opin
palaav *occupy (something) as if* *one owns it*	palaav
pudong *put down*	pudong

qwaaril *quarrel*	qwaaril
ryet *rate*	ryet
saach *search*	saach
shub *shove*	shub
sidong *sit; sit down*	sidong
suolla *swallow*	suolla
tan-op *stand; stand up*	tan-op
tomp *punch*	tomp
uon *own*	uon
vuot *vote*	vuot
wain *rotate hips*	wain

Verbs	*Present Continuous Tense*
aada *order*	a aada; aada-in
aks *ask*	a aks; aks-in
ansa *answer*	a ansa; ansa-in
baak *bark*	a baak; baak-in
barro *borrow*	a barro; barro-in
bi *be*	a bi; E. being
brok *break*	a brok; brok-in
byed *bathe*	a byed; byed-in
chaaj *charge*	a chaaj; chaaj-in
chaka-chaka *mess up*	a chaka-chaka; chaka-chaka-in
chrech *stretch*	a chrech; chrech-in
chuo *throw*	a chuo; chuo-in
dash-weh *throw away*	a dash-weh; dash-weh-in
distraah *destroy*	a distraah; distraah-in
duh *do*	a duh; duh-in

enta *enter*	a enta; enta-in
expek *expect*	a expek; expect-in
faam *farm*	a faam; faam-in
figet *forget*	a figet; figet-in
fren-op *make up with;* *make oneself friendly to*	a fren-op
gi *give*	a gi; gi-in; E. giving
goh *go*	a goh; goh-in
ha *have*	a ha; E. having
hag-op *handle roughly;* *speak harshly to*	a hag-op; hag-op-in
hoks *hack; husk*	a hoks; hoks-in
infek *infect*	a infek; infek-in
iyem *aim*	a iyem; iyem-in
jaah *draw; pull*	a jaah; jaah-in
juk *prick*	a juk; juk-in
ketch *catch*	a ketch; ketch-in
konk *hit with sharp blow*	a konk; konk-in
laas *lose*	a laas; laas-in
laba *talk excessively*	a laba; laba-in
lef *leave*	a lef; lef-in
maach *march*	a maach; maach-in
myel *mail*	a myel; myel-in
nyem *name*	a nyem; nyem-in
opin *open*	a opin; opin-in
palaav *occupy (something)* *as if one owns it*	a palaav; palaav-in
pudong *put down*	a pudong; pudong-in
qwaaril *quarrel*	a qwaaril; qwaaril-in

ryet *rate*	a ryet; ryet-in
saach *search*	a saach; saach-in
shub *shove*	a shub; shub-in
sidong *sit; sit down*	sidong; sidong-in
suolla *swallow*	a suolla; suolla-in
tan-op *stand; stand up*	tan-op; tan-op-in
tomp *punch*	a tomp; tomp-in
uon *own*	a uon; uon-in
vuot *vote*	a vuot; vuot-in
wain *rotate hips*	a wain; wain-in

Verbs	*Past Tense*

(Note that *did* is sometimes replaced with *beeh, weeh, beeh did,* or *weeh did,* e.g., *beeh aada, weeh aada, beeh did aada,* or *weeh did aada.* The verb *bi* is addressed separately. All the conjugations for the verb *bi* are outlined below.)

aada *order*	did aada; aada
aks *ask*	did aks; aks
ansa *ansa*	did ansa; ansa
baak *bark*	did baak; baak
barro *borrow*	did barro; barro
bi *be*	did a (a did; ben a; wen a; beeh did a; weeh did a); did deh (beeh deh; weeh deh; beeh did deh; weeh did deh); did bi (beeh bi; weeh bi; beeh did bi; weeh did bi)
brok *break*	did brok; brok
byed *bathe*	did byed; byed

141

chaaj *charge*	did chaaj; chaaj
chaka-chaka *mess up*	did chaka-chaka; chaka-chaka
chrech *stretch*	did chrech; chrech
chuo *throw*	did chuo; chuo
dash-weh *throw away*	did dash-weh; dash-weh
distraah *destroy*	did distraah; distraah
duh *do*	did duh; duh
enta *enter*	did enta; enta
expek *expect*	did expek; expek
faam *farm*	did faam; faam
figet *forget*	did figet; figet
fren-op *make up with; make oneself friendly to*	did fren-op; fren-op
gi *give*	did gi; gi
goh *go*	did goh; goh
ha *have*	did ha; ha
hag-op *handle roughly; speak harshly to*	did hag-op; hag-og
hoks *hack; husk*	did hoks; hoks
infek *infect*	did infek; infek
iyem *aim*	did iyem; iyem
jaah *draw; pull*	did jaah; jaah
juk *prick*	did juk; juk
ketch *catch*	did ketch; ketch
konk *hit with sharp blow*	did konk; konk
laas *lose*	did laas; laas
laba *talk excessively*	did laba; laba
lef *leave*	did lef; lef
maach *march*	did maach; maach

myel *mail*	did myel; myel
nyem *name*	did nyem; nyem
opin *open*	did opin; opin
palaav *occupy (something) as if one owns it*	did palaav; palaav
pudong *put down*	did pudong; pudong
qwaaril *quarrel*	did qwaaril; qwaaril
ryet *rate*	did ryet; ryet
saach *search*	did saach; saach
shub *shove*	did shub; shub
sidong *sit; sit down*	did sidong; sidong
suolla *swallow*	did suolla; suolla
tan-op *stand; stand up*	did tan-op; tan-op
tomp *punch*	did tomp; tomp
uon *own*	did uon; uon
vuot *vote*	did vuot; vuot
wain *rotate hips*	did wain; wain

Verbs	*Continuous Past/Continuous Past Perfect Tense*

(Note that *did a* is sometimes replaced with *ben a, wen a, did deh, beeh deh, weeh deh, beeh did deh,* or *weeh did deh,* e.g., *ben a aada, wen a aada, beeh deh aada, weeh deh aada, beeh did deh aada,* or *weeh did deh aada. Sidong* and *tan-op* are exceptions. Their conjugations are outlined below.)

aada *order*	did a aada
aks *ask*	did a aks
ansa *ansa*	did a ansa
baak *bark*	did a baak
barro *borrow*	did a barro

bi *be*	did a bi
brok *break*	did a brok
byed *bathe*	did a byed
chaaj *charge*	did a chaaj
chaka-chaka *mess up*	did a chaka-chaka
chrech *stretch*	did a chrech
chuo *throw*	did a chuo
dash-weh *throw away*	did a dash-weh
distraah *destroy*	did a distraah
duh *do*	did a duh
enta *enter*	did a enta
expek *expect*	did a expek
faam *farm*	did a faam
figet *forget*	did a figet
fren-op *make up with;*	did a fren-op
make oneself friendly to	
gi *give*	did a gi
goh *go*	did a goh
ha *have*	did a ha
hag-op *handle roughly;*	did a hag-op
speak harshly to	
hoks *hack; husk*	did a hoks
infek *infect*	did a infek
iyem *aim*	did a iyem
jaah *draw; pull*	did a jaah
juk *prick*	did a juk
ketch *catch*	did a ketch
konk *hit with sharp blow*	did a konk
laas *lose*	did a laas

laba *talk excessively*	did a laba
lef *leave*	did a lef
maach *march*	did a maach
myel *mail*	did a myel
nyem *name*	did a nyem
opin *open*	did a opin
palaav *occupy (something) as if one owns it*	did a palaav
pudong *put down*	did a pudong
qwaaril *quarrel*	did a qwaaril
ryet *rate*	did a ryet
saach *search*	did a saach
shub *shove*	did a shub
sidong *sit; sit down*	did sidong; beeh sidong; weeh sidong; beeh did sidong; weeh did sidong
suolla *swallow*	did a suolla
tan-op *stand; stand up*	did tan-op; beeh tan-op; weeh tan-op; beeh did tan-op; weeh did tan-op
tomp *punch*	did a tomp
uon *own*	did a uon
vuot *vote*	did a vuot
wain *rotate hips*	did a wain

Verbs	Present Perfect Tense
aada *order*	aada
aks *ask*	aks
ansa *answer*	ansa
baak *bark*	baak
barro *borrow*	barro
bi *be*	a; deh; E. been
brok *break*	brok
byed *bathe*	byed
chaaj *charge*	chaaj
chaka-chaka *mess up*	chaka-chaka
chrech *stretch*	chrech
chuo *throw*	chuo
dash-weh *throw away*	dash-weh
distraah *destroy*	distraah
duh *do*	duh; E. done
enta *enter*	enta
expek *expect*	expek
faam *farm*	faam
figet *forget*	figet
fren-op *make up with; make oneself friendly to*	fren-op
gi *give*	gi
goh *go*	E. gone
ha *have*	ha
hag-op *handle roughly; speak harshly to*	hag-op
hoks *hack; husk*	hoks

infek *infect*	infek
iyem *aim*	iyem
jaah *draw; pull*	jaah
juk *prick*	juk
ketch *catch*	ketch
konk *hit with sharp blow*	konk
laas *lose*	laas
laba *talk excesively*	laba
lef *leave*	lef
maach *march*	maach
myel *mail*	myel
nyem *name*	nyem
opin *open*	opin
palaav *occupy (something) as if one owns it*	palaav
pudong *put down*	pudong
qwaaril *quarrel*	qwaaril
ryet *rate*	ryet
saach *search*	saach
sidong *sit; sit down*	sidong
shub *shove*	shub
suolla *swallow*	suolla
tan-op *stand; stand up*	tan-op
tomp *punch*	tomp
uon *own*	uon
vuot *vote*	vuot
wain *rotate hips*	wain

Verbs	*Past Perfect Tense*

(Note that *did* is sometimes replaced with *beeh, weeh, beeh did,* or *weeh did,* e.g., *beeh aada, weeh aada, beeh did aada,* or *weeh did aada.* The verb *bi* is addressed separately. All the conjugations for the verb *bi* are outlined below.)

aada *order*	did aada
aks *ask*	did aks
ansa *answer*	did ansa
baak *bark*	did baak
barro *borrow*	did barro
bi *be*	did a (a did; ben a; wen a; beeh did a; weeh did a); did deh (beeh deh; weeh deh; beeh did deh; weeh did deh); did bi (beeh bi; weeh bi; beeh did bi; weeh did bi)
brok *break*	did brok
byed *bathe*	did byed
chaaj *charge*	did chaaj
chaka-chaka *mess up*	did chaka-chaka
chrech *stretch*	did chrech
chuo *throw*	did chuo
dash-weh *throw away*	did dash-weh
distraah *destroy*	did distraah
duh *do*	did duh
enta *enter*	did enta
expek *expect*	did expek
faam *farm*	did faam

figet *forget*	did figet
fren-op *make up with;* *make oneself friendly to*	did fren-op
gi *give*	did gi
goh *go*	did goh; E. did gone
ha *have*	did ha
hag-op *handle roughly;* *speak harshly to*	did hag-op
hoks *hack; husk*	did hoks
infek *infect*	did infek
iyem *aim*	did iyem
jaah *draw; pull*	did jaah
juk *prick*	did juk
ketch *catch*	did ketch
konk *hit with sharp blow*	did konk
laas *lose*	did laas
laba *talk excesively*	did laba
lef *leave*	did lef
maach *march*	did maach
myel *mail*	did myel
nyem *name*	did nyem
opin *open*	did opin
palaav *occupy (something)* *as if one owns it*	did palaav
pudong *put down*	did pudong
qwaaril *quarrel*	did qwaaril
ryet *rate*	did ryet
saach *search*	did saach
sidong *sit; sit down*	did sidong

shub *shove*	did shub
suolla *swallow*	did suolla
tan-op *stand; stand up*	did tan-op
tomp *punch*	did tomp
uon *own*	did uon
vuot *vote*	did vuot
wain *rotate hips*	did wain

Verbs	*Continuous Present Perfect Tense*
aada *order*	aada; E. been aada-in
aks *ask*	aks; E. been aks-in
ansa *answer*	ansa; E. been ansa-in
baak *bark*	baak; E. been baak-in
barro *borrow*	barro; E. been barro-in
bi *be*	a; deh; E. been
brok *break*	brok; E. been brok-in
byed *bathe*	byed; E. been byed-in
chaaj *charge*	chaaj; E. been chaaj-in
chaka-chaka *mess up*	chaka-chaka; E. been chaka-chaka-in
chrech *stretch*	chrech; E. been chrech-in
chuo *throw*	chuo; E. been chuo-in
dash-weh *throw away*	dash-weh; E. been dash-weh-in
distraah *destroy*	distraah; E. been distraah-in
duh *do*	duh; done; E. been doing
enta *enter*	enta; E. been enta-in
expek *expect*	expek; E. been expek-in
faam *farm*	faam; E. been faam-in
figet *forget*	figet; E. been figet-in

fren-op *make up with;*
make oneself friendly to

fren-op; E. been fren-op-in

gi *give*

gi; E. been gi-in; E.
been giving

goh *go*

E. gone; E. been goh-in

ha *have*

ha; E. been having

hag-op *handle roughly;*
speak harshly to

hag-op; E. been hag-op-in

hoks *hack; husk*

hoks; E. been hoks-in

infek *infect*

infek; E. been infek-in

iyem *aim*

iyem; E. been iyem-in

jaah *draw; pull*

jaah; E. been jaah-in

juk *prick*

juk; E. been juk-in

ketch *catch*

ketch; E. been ketch-in

konk *hit with sharp blow*

konk; E. been konk-in

laas *lose*

laas; E. been laas-in

laba *talk excesively*

laba; E. been laba-in

lef *leave*

lef; E. been lef-in

maach *march*

maach; E. been maach-in

myel *mail*

myel; E. been myel-in

nyem *name*

nyem; E. been nyem-in

opin *open*

opin; E. been opin-in

palaav *occupy (something)*
as if one owns it

palaav; E. been palaav-in

pudong *put down*

pudong; E. been pudong-in

qwaaril *quarrel*

qwaaril; E. been qwaaril-in

ryet *rate*

ryet; E. been ryet-in

saach *search*

saach; E. been saach-in

sidong *sit; sit down*

sidong; E. been sidong-in

shub *shove*	shub; E. been shub-in
suolla *swallow*	suolla; E. been suolla-in
tan-op *stand; stand up*	tan-op; E. been tan-op-in
tomp *punch*	tomp; E. been tomp-in
uon *own*	uon; E. been uon-in
vuot *vote*	vuot; E. been vuot-in
wain *rotate hips*	wain; E. been wain-in

Verbs	*Future Tense*
aada *order*	aggo aada; gweeh aada
aks *ask*	aggo aks; gweeh aks
ansa *answer*	aggo ansa; gweeh ansa
baak *bark*	aggo baak; gweeh baak
barro *borrow*	aggo barro; gweeh barro
bi *be*	aggo bi; gweeh bi; aggo deh; gweeh deh
brok *break*	aggo brok; gweeh brok
byed *bathe*	aggo byed; gweeh byed
chaaj *charge*	aggo chaaj; gweeh chaaj
chaka-chaka *mess up*	aggo chaka-chaka gweeh chaka- chaka
chrech *stretch*	aggo chrech; gweeh chrech
chuo *throw*	aggo chuo; gweeh chuo
dash-weh *throw away*	aggo dash-weh; gweeh dash-weh
distraah *destroy*	aggo distraah; gweeh distraah
duh *do*	aggo duh; gweeh duh
enta *enter*	aggo enta; gweeh enta
expek *expect*	aggo expek; gweeh expek

faam *farm*	aggo faam; gweeh faam
figet *forget*	aggo figet; gweeh figet
fren-op *make up with; make oneself friendly to*	aggo fren-op; gweeh fren-op
gi *give*	aggo gi; gweeh gi
goh *go*	aggo goh; gweeh goh
ha *have*	aggo ha; gweeh ha
hag-op *handle roughly; speak harshly to*	aggo hag-op; gweeh hag-op
hoks *hack; husk*	aggo hoks; gweeh hoks
infek *infect*	aggo infek; gweeh infek
iyem *aim*	aggo iyem; gweeh iyem
jaah *draw; pull*	aggo jaah; gweeh jaah
juk *prick*	aggo juk; gweeh juk
ketch *catch*	aggo ketch; gweeh ketch
konk *hit with sharp blow*	aggo konk; gweeh konk
laas *lose*	aggo laas; gweeh laas
laba *talk excessively*	aggo laba; gweeh laba
lef *leave*	aggo lef; gweeh lef
maach *march*	aggo maach; gweeh maach
myel *mail*	aggo myel; gweeh myel
nyem *name*	aggo nyem; gweeh nyem
opin *open*	aggo opin; gweeh opin
palaav *occupy (something) as if one owns it*	aggo palaav; gweeh palaav
pudong *put down*	aggo pudong; gweeh pudong
qwaaril *quarrel*	aggo qwaaril; gweeh qwaaril
ryet *rate*	aggo ryet; gweeh ryet
saach *search*	aggo saach; gweeh saach

shub *shove*	aggo shub; gweeh shub
sidong *sit; sit down*	aggo sidong; gweeh sidong
suolla *swallow*	aggo suolla; gweeh suolla
tan-op *stand; stand up*	aggo tan-op; gweeh tan-op
tomp *punch*	aggo tomp; gweeh tomp
uon *own*	aggo uon; gweeh uon
vuot *vote*	aggo vuot; gweeh vuot
wain *rotate hips*	aggo wain; gweeh wain

Verbs	*Conditional Future Tense*
aada *order*	wi aada; wudda aada
aks *ask*	wi aks; wudda aks
ansa *answer*	wi ansa; wudda ansa
baak *bark*	wi baak; wudda baak
barro *borrow*	wi barro; wudda barro
bi *be*	wi bi; wudda bi; wi deh; wudda deh
brok *break*	wi brok; wudda brok
byed *bathe*	wi byed; wudda byed
chaaj *charge*	wi chaaj; wudda chaaj
chaka-chaka *mess up*	wi chaka-chaka; wudda chaka- chaka
chrech *stretch*	wi chech; wudda chrech
chuo *throw*	wi chuo; wudda chuo
dash-weh *throw away*	wi dash-weh; wudda dash-weh
distraah *destroy*	wi distraah; wudda distraah
duh *do*	wi duh; wudda duh
enta *enter*	wi enta; wudda enta
expek *expect*	wi expek; wudda expek

faam *farm* — wi faam; wudda faam

figet *forget* — wi figet; wudda figet

fren-op *make up with;* — wi fren-op; wudda fren-op
make oneself friendly to

gi *give* — wi gi; wudda gi

goh *go* — wi goh; wudda goh

ha *have* — wi ha; wudda ha

hag-op *handle roughly;* — wi hag-op; wudda hag-op
speak harshly to

hoks *hack; husk* — wi hoks; wudda hoks

infek *infect* — wi infek; wudda infek

iyem *aim* — wi iyem; wudda iyem

jaah *draw; pull* — wi jaah; wudda jaah

juk *prick* — wi juk; wudda juk

ketch *catch* — wi ketch; wudda ketch

konk *hit with sharp blow* — wi konk; wudda konk

laas *lose* — wi laas; wudda laas

laba *talk excessively* — wi laba; wudda laba

lef *leave* — wi lef; wudda lef

maach *march* — wi maach; wudda maach

myel *mail* — wi myel; wudda myel

nyem *name* — wi nyem; wudda nyem

opin *open* — wi opin; wudda opin

palaav *occupy (something)* — wi palaav; wudda palaav
as if one owns it

pudong *put down* — wi pudong; wudda pudong

qwaaril *quarrel* — wi qwaaril; wudda qwaaril

ryet *rate* — wi ryet; wudda ryet

saach *search* — wi saach; wudda saach

shub *shove*	wi shub; wudda shub
sidong *sit; sit down*	wi sidong; wudda sidong
suolla *swallow*	wi suolla; wudda suolla
tan-op *stand; stand up*	wi tan-op; wudda tan-op
tomp *punch*	wi tomp; wudda tomp
uon *own*	wi uon; wudda uon
vuot *vote*	wi vuot; wudda vuot
wain *rotate hips*	wi wain; wudda wain

References

Cassidy, F.G. (1957). Iteration as a word-Forming device in Jamaican folk speech. American English, 32, p. 49-53.

Gladwell, M (1994). The creole creation. The Washington Post. Retrieved from https://www.washingtonpost.com/archive/opinions/1994/05/15/the-creole-creation/90900fef-5d8f-4c5c-800b-ef5db82eca6e/?utm_term=.06ca35146856

Madden, R. (2009). The historical and culture aspects of Jamaican Patois. Retrieved from https://debate.uvm.edu/dreadlibrary/Madden.htm

About the Author

The author was born in Jamaica and grew up in the cool hills of Clarendon. Despite working in the field of psychology, writing has remained one of her greatest passions, and she indulges in both fictional and non-fictional works. The author has the desire to see Jamaican Creole legitimized as a language. The author hopes that her current work will aid in that process.

Made in the USA
Las Vegas, NV
08 November 2023